The
Art of
Nurturing

THE ART OF
Nurturing

On the Job Training
For Parents and Teachers
In Adult/Child Relationships

E. E. White

Santa Cruz School District
Santa Cruz, California

Peek Publications • Box 11065 • Palo Alto, California 94306

ISBN 0-917962-42-7

Manufactured in the United States of America

Preface

This book is based on the idea that there is no more creative and important job in the world than nurturing the growth of human beings. The quality of a society's future is dependent upon the quality of the relationships and discipline experienced by its children. Parents and teachers have a very great effect on the kind of person a child becomes.

The *Art of Nurturing* is intended to be a training experience for the reader. It can be used individually, with a friend, or with groups.

Each chapter has a series of exercises to help make the total reading/ learning experience more meaningful and lasting. If you want to get an overview of the subject matter, you might just think through the exercises without really doing them. If you want to get more than an overview, you might do the exercises on your own. If you want a little deeper experience, you might choose to do the exercises with a partner. If you want to receive the benefits of sharing experiences of adult-child relationships, you could organize a "coffee klatch" of friends to review the ideas and exercises together. The book could also be used by a group leader as a resource for in-service training with teachers and/or parents. Basically *The Art of Nurturing* is intended to be a flexible book which fits a variety of learning experiences for adults and presents ideas and experiences which leave the final choices up to the learner.

Dedication

This book, a synthesis of my thoughts and experiences, has been greatly influenced by these three sources: (1) my family; (2) the teachers, students, and parents in the schools in which I have worked for the past several years; (3) teachers in the field of human relationships.

My wife, Gayle, and our children, Brent and Brian, have been the basis for understanding and experiencing the nuances of human relationships. There is nothing like daily living together to distinguish impractical from realistic ideas.

Schools also pull me back to reality, because they tend to generally reflect our society and are a microcosm of the world. As difficult as working in public schools can be, one of its redeeming qualities is that meaningful confrontations between people and groups occur.

Haim Ginott,[1] Thomas Gordon,[2] and Gerald Patterson[3] have been the authors who have helped me considerably to understand adult/child relationships. I identified so closely with Haim Ginott's ideas that although we never met, I felt I had lost a personal friend when he died. Thomas Gordon provided my training and part-time employment as a teacher of Parent Effectiveness Training. Seminars and books by Gerald Patterson have helped me to understand that reinforcement is an integral, unavoidable part of relationship.

Virginia Satir,[4] Harris Clemes, and Renald Bean have had a strong influence on the style of this book. Many ideas in the chapters on "Self-Esteem" and "Resolving the Dilemmas We Face" were inspired by Harris and Renald (consultants from the Santa Cruz Association for Personal and Organizational Development). Richard Schmuck[5] of Organization Development Consultants in Eugene, Oregon, provided a framework of human relationships from which to synthesize life's options.

Authors whose ideas have contributed to THE ART OF NURTURING are listed under References in the order their names or ideas first appear.

Contents

Self-Concept and Self-Esteem

What do these students have in common?

(1) Scott thinks he is the "dumbest" kid in the class. He still wants to learn but he often just gives up because he has felt the pain of failure so many times.

(2) Laura tries to win the friendship of her peers by frequently giving them candy which she has stolen. For a long time she has believed that she needs to do something extra to get people to like her.

(3) Jack is constantly involved in unprovoked fights. He seems to need to prove he is the toughest boy on the block.

(4) Armondo is a very capable student who tries too hard. He gets so nervous about tests he often misreads the questions and makes mistakes. He feels the single reason he is accepted by others is because he is "smart."

(5) Ben will not play with other children. During recess he can usually be found alone at the far corner of the playground. He has turned down many offers of friendship because he is afraid his peers will not like him, once they know him.

(6) Betty is more than affectionate with all her dates. The only way that she has ever sensed the individual attention of another human being is through intimacy in temporary relationships.

(7) Dan is the best football player on the practice field, but he seldom does well in actual games. He has never thought he had the ability to perform under pressure.

(8) Juanita spends hours each morning primping in the mirror. She is a pretty girl who thinks the only reason people like her is because of the way she looks.

(9) Ted works after school and on the weekends. He doesn't really need all the money he earns, but feels that without a fancy car, nice clothes and extra spending money he is "nothing."

All of these students have one thing in common—they are extremely unsure of themselves, a feeling many people have. The irony is that this epidemic of human misery can be prevented.

Relationship and discipline help determine how a child feels about himself. In turn, a child's attitude toward feelings and advice of others is strongly affected by how he or she perceives, and feels about self. The terms used most frequently to describe this belief and feeling are "self-concept" and "self-esteem." The next two chapters may help you decide your options for relationship and discipline, or the spirit with which you implement the options that best fit your situation.

The terms self-concept and self-esteem refer basically to whom a person thinks she or he is and how one feels about it. The most important part is how one feels about it. Self-esteem basically means the same thing as self-confidence or attitude about self. The person with positive self-esteem can usually say, "I am glad I am me." Briggs[6] defines the concept as, "Self-esteem is not noisy conceit. It is quiet self-respect, a feeling of self-worth."

When a person basically feels positive about onself, it is like having a constantly replenishing basket full of food. The person with a brimming, refilling basket of food can easily give to others who are hungry, but one who is starving and fears the basket will be empty finds it difficult or impossible to consider the hunger of others except when reciprocation is anticipated. This sentence would be equally true if you replaced the word "food" with the word "love." Try it again with the word "love" and see if it has meaning.

Self-esteem affects learning, respecting, loving, giving, accomplishing, following and leading. The degree to which one can grow to be caring, independent, and full-functioning in life often is directly related to the degree of one's positive self-esteem. How one feels about self affects how one lives his or her life. Positive self-esteem is based on one's belief that she or he is both worthwhile and loveable. Where does a person get this kind of belief in self? Adults who were asked this question answered:

"My parents just plain liked me as well as loved me, and I knew it."

"My father always put me down but somehow my mother had a way of getting across to me that I was a very special person."

"There was one teacher I had who seemed to be able to see through all my faults and appreciate my strengths."

"From people whom I respect highly but at the same time get a sense of equal relationship with them. It's like they think what I have to say and what I feel is important to them."

"From feeling that I am in control of what happens to me. It's like knowing that I am safe."

"When I accomplish something that is important to me a little voice inside of me says, 'You did it! You did it!'"

"I used to go up and down depending upon whether I got a lot of recognition from other people. The ups never seemed to last and the downs were unending. Professional counseling helped to change that for me. Now from within I know I am an OK person most of the time. The reactions of others are still wanted but they are no longer the most important thing."

As nurturers, adults want children to feel good about themselves, and the most stable kind of self-esteem comes from within. To develop that feeling, children are strongly affected by the input from significant people in their environment.

Each person values self to the degree that she or he has been valued.[6]

The major factors that influence self-esteem are (1) the amount of respectful, accepting, concerned treatment an individual receives from the significant others in one's life, and (2) the individual's history of successes in comparison to the standards one has set for oneself.

Coopersmith[7] found three characteristics in families that produced children of high self-esteem.

1. The families were very warm, affectionate, and physically expressed their affection for their children.
2. The families had some way of communicating to a child a respect for him or her as a unique person.
3. The families had very stable and clear limits which were consistently enforced without extreme harshness. The limits were realistic and fair. There was also room for choices, individual expression, and discussion.

Understanding what makes up a specific child's self-concept and self-esteem, and what can be done to enhance them can increase the nurturer's influence on a child's positive feelings about self.

The *self-concept* of an individual is very resistant to change. It generally is one's self-identity. There are many things that are central to one's self-concept and other things that are a part of it that are not quite as important to the person as the central identities.[8]

Self-esteem is the way a person feels about his or her self-concept. Self-esteem can go up and down depending upon the discrepancy between performance and standards. An example could be that of a girl who might have central to her self-concept that she is an artist. Her self-esteem is her feelings about what kind of an artist she is. She might have a low self-esteem if she feels that she is a very poor artist and positive self-esteem if she feels the level of her artistic competency meets the standards that she has set for herself (often influenced by the reality of the standards that significant others set for her).

An adult who hopes to help a child increase in self-esteem, should be aware of those things which make up the child's self-concept. One way of doing this is to list all the positive or neutral things you can think of that describe a specific child (i.e., dancer, learner, enthusiastic, curious, etc.). Use the space for this purpose:

The descriptions of a child can usually be divided into two main areas:[8]
1. What a child thinks he is (called categories).
2. The positive ways in which a child is unique (called attributes).

The following is an example of how one parent divided the descriptions of a child into these areas:

AREAS OF SELF-CONCEPT

What the child thinks he or she is (categories)	How the child is unique (attributes
(I,5) Son	(I,5) Coordinated—learns new sports easily
(M,5) Brother	
(I,5) Athlete	(I,5) Outgoing—likes people
(I,5) Football player	(I,5) Friendly—makes friends easily, talks readily
(I,5) Student	
(S,4) Writer	(M,5) Strong—almost unstoppable when incensed
(M,4) Joker	
(S,3) Christian	(M,4) Humorous—appreciates hearing and telling jokes
(I,5) American	
(M,5) Scientist	(I,5) Caring—tries to help others when they are hurting
	(S,2) Sensitive—hurts easily and deeply, enjoys intensely
	(I,5) Curious—experiments; questtions a lot.

Exercise #1

Use your list as a starter and on the form below for one of your children (or if you are a teacher, one of your students), list the categories and attributes which fit that specific child. Elaborate on the attributes, as in the previus example.

AREAS OF SELF-CONCEPT

What the child thinks he or she is (categories)	The child's positive and unique characteristics (attributes)

In Exercise #1 you described your impressions of the child's self-concept. Self-concept is a fairly stable part of an individual and is formed throughout life (for the most part in the early years) by the experiences, adult models, and environment to which an individual is exposed. As was said earlier, some parts of an individual's self-concept are intensely important to him. Other parts are moderately important and some are only slightly important.

Exercise #2

Look at the descriptions you listed in Exercise #1. Which of the categories and attributes listed are seen by the child as intensely important (I), moderately important (M), or slightly important (S). Put a letter by each item listed to indicate the level of importance as you imagine the child sees it.

You now have an idea of the parts (categories and attributes) that make up a specific child's self-concept and their relative importance to the child. Effectiveness in coping with life depends on how well a person thinks he or she is functioning in each of those areas—particularly those which are perceived as intensely important. You can determine whether the individual feelings of self-esteem are generally low or generally positive by rating each of the parts that make up the child's self-concept.

Exercise #3

To determine the level of self-esteem of the specific child in Exercise #1, return to that exercise again and put a number beside each category and attribute to indicate the level of self-esteem you think the child has in each area of self-concept. Put 1 for "always feels low" in this area; 2 for "usually feels low"; 3 for "sometimes feels positive"; 4 for "usually feels positive"; 5 for "always feels positive."

You now have an indication of your impressions of a specific child's levels of self-esteem in each area of self-concept. For those areas that are generally low, you will want to find ways to increase the child's self-esteem. For those areas that are generally positive, you will want to find ways to support the positiveness to assure that it will continue. If time and energy are a problem, give priority to those areas you rated as "I" (perceived by the child as intensely important). Research has indicated that when a person increases in self-esteem in an area central to self-concept, this increase has a generalizing effect to other parts of self-concept,[8] i.e., the child who sees him or herself as an artist may increase in feelings about total self, if one accomplishes at the level of standard that he or she has set in artistic activities.

Before finding ways to increase or support self-esteem areas of self-concept, try the following exercises to help determine the validity of your impressions.

Exercise #4

For a couple of days, set aside about ten to thirty minutes to observe the child described in Exercise #1 while he/she is doing something that does not involve you. Do you notice any categories or attributes you haven't listed?

Exercise #5

Talk with the child about Exercises #1-3 to determine if there are differences in adult/child perceptions of the categories and attributes listed and their ratings.

Exercise #6

Ask the child how much is expected (standards) of him/her in the categories by the child and by you. Is there a difference?

Increasing Self-Esteem: How You and the Child Can Really Enjoy Each Other

As mentioned in the previous chapter, the two major factors that influence self-esteem are: (1) the amount of respectful, accepting, concerned treatment an individual receives from significant others in the environment, and, (2) the individual's history of successes. Self-esteem related to the self-concept attributes is strongly affected by factor #1. Self-esteem related to the self-concept categories is strongly affected by factor #2.

Three avenues through which one could enhance self-esteem in self-concept categories are:

1. arranging the environment for success.
2. providing experiences which will increase skill.
3. valuing the child's interests and activities.

First, a **caution** will be explored. The standard that a child sets for himself in any self-concept category is greatly influenced by the standards that are communicated to him by significant persons in his environment. An adult who wants to help a child increase his self-esteem in a self-concept category area, should avoid over-emphasizing that particular area to the degree that it becomes bigger than life to the child.

The best way to avoid over-emphasis in a specific area is to be continually aware of the present degree of interest the child has in this area. Respond to the child at the level of his or her interest and not the level of the adult's interest. Be prepared to stop all attention and activities in the specific area if the child's interests suddenly change. Most importantly, let the child lead the way to the amount of involvement he or she wants. Be careful not to change your positive influence on a child's self-esteem to pressure for success.

Wally Trabing, a columnist for the *Santa Cruz Sentinel*, wrote this poem about a mother of a handicapped child:

7

Don't Let a Year Get in Your Way

The year is waning, yet not,
For years tell of time, and there is work to do and we should not set up these
    fences.
The child is still a child.
Our love is still a love.
Despite the year.
It should not be a wall, a comparison, a limit.
It will pass, for there are no limits.
I chide this lady beside me who talks of her child.
Measuring the year, impatiently, as if it is measuring her in the eyes of her child.
"Yes," she says, "There was progress," reluctantly, "but not enough."
I am an outsider listening.
Saying, "You're doin' all right."
I can sense the picture; your fluid love that pushes you beyond the failure of
    time sections.
I know, a poem is no help.
But it says keep on.
Don't let a year get in your way.

The following example could be appropriate or inappropriate, depending upon the degree and consistency of interest of the child involved. We will assume that the child's interest is intense and that the adult is following the child's lead in providing attention and activities. Let's say the child is a boy who aspires to be an athlete, especially a baseball player. Presently this area of self-concept seems intensely important to him. The adult decides to do everything possible to enhance feelings of positive self-esteem. The three avenues listed previously could be used.

The adult might arrange the environment for success by first playing catch and batting with a large plastic bat and ball, throwing the ball slowly at short distances and helping the child hold and swing the bat. If there are no children nearby in the neighborhood who are of about the same ability, the adult would seek out children of the child's level to frequently play with him.

The adult would provide experiences to increase skill by teaching the child (informally practicing with him without pressure) to throw, catch, bat, and so on.

The adult would give value to the self-concept area by expressing appreciation, for example: "I get a lot of pleasure from playing catch with you," "It looks like you enjoy playing catch, too." "I enjoy seeing you have fun playing baseball," "Thanks for showing me your new pitch, it's exciting to see the new things you are learning," "It seems like you are pretty excited about the things you are learning, too," "I really enjoyed your telling me about the ball game you had at recess, it sounds like you really felt good about how your team did."

Note that the adult avoided the trap of placing impossible-to-achieve labels on the child. It would have been tempting to say things like "You're the best ball player on the block" or "You're a great athlete." If a child is not a great athlete he may not receive messages like this as sincere and if he hears it often enough, he may struggle to become a great athlete while feeling unappreciated because he is not great enough. (For further information regarding "New Ways of Praise," refer to Ginott's[1] second chapter, pgs. 37-52.)

An adult's comments to a child will be on target and enhancing if the following principle is kept in mind—*a person wants basically to be appreciated for one's existence on this earth, for one's experiences in one's world, and one's feelings about those experiences.* Appreciation is more effectively communicated when a statement focuses on the experience itself and the feelings about that experience rather than an aptitude or ability of the person.

Exercise #1

For the child in Exercise #1 in the previous chapter, list the things that you have been doing that would enhance self-esteem in the categories area of self-concept. Also list the things you would like to do but haven't started yet.

ENHANCING SELF-ESTEEM IN THE CATEGORIES AREA

Things I have done or am doing	Things I would like to do in the near future

Enhancing Self-Esteem In The Attributes Area

As mentioned earlier, the attribute areas of self-concept are strongly affected by the amount and kind of respectful, accepting, concerned treatment an individual receives from the significant people in his life. Of this, intense "concerned treatment" (or cherishing) is the most important ingredient. According to Briggs:[6]

> Children survive on acceptance but they do not blossom on it. They need something stronger. They need *cherishing*, they must feel valued and precious and special just because they exist. Then deep down they can like who they are.
>
> Cherishing is not something you necessarily give lip service to; rather it is the feeling you have towards a child. It is sensing uniqueness and finding it dear. In spite of intermittent irritations, you remain open to the wonder of the child.

In an unpublished song, Betty Reed succinctly says: "The truth is in being, not merely becoming."

In this author's opinion, being cherished by at least one person is the cornerstone to positive self-esteem. For some, a belief that "God loves me" helps compensate for cherishing not received from significant others. Knowing that you are really loved by another human being is the basic ingredient of living. Some are fortunate to find this early in life; however, most spend a lifetime of frustration, searching for that special person who will cherish them and become engrossed in them. The significant adults in a child's life can assure that he or she will be among the fortunate ones by communicating cherishing through taking a little time each day to be totally engrossed in the child. The adult's actions, affection, and words are a large part of this.

Look at the unique attributes you listed in Exercise #1 in the preceding chapter. How aware is the child of these unique qualities? Does the child know he/she is cherished in these areas? How do you communicate to the child that he/she is cherished? What actions do you take in this direction? How do you show affection for the child? Do you have some very special things you say to him/her from time to time?

Affectionate words can be very important, although sometimes it is hard to find words to match our feelings. The American Greeting Card Company[9] has developed a series of cards for the specific use of an adult to communicate cherishment to a child. Here are some of the sayings on the cards:

> I've meant to tell you many times before . . . how much I enjoy the times we've spent together.
>
> You're already famous . . . I tell everybody about you.
>
> When I don't see you, even for just one day . . . I miss you.
>
> When you grow up . . . I'll miss the way you are right now.
>
> I'd like you a lot . . . even if you weren't my kid.
>
> You do a lot of things that bring me joy.

You're the kind of kid I always wanted to be.

You're really great . . . I couldn't have created a better person.

When I look at you . . . I'm proud and happy with what I see.

I'm glad you're a part of my world.

The day you were born was one of the happiest days of my life (and it still is!).

I just wanted to tell you: you've brought so much happiness to my life.

You know what makes today special? . . . YOU!!

There is no one else exactly like you . . . not in the whole world.

You know something? You make my whole world so beautiful and meaningful with your joys and sorrows.

I'll always be your friend . . . and I just want to be sure you know that.

I probably should say it more often . . . I'm proud of you.

You're trying very hard . . . and I just want you to know that I've noticed.

Keep it up . . . you're doing just great.

You may not want to talk about it now—but whenever you need someone to listen, I'm here.

It wasn't luck . . . you made it happen.

Exercise #2

For the child in Exercise #1, list the actions, demonstrations of affection, and words you communicate.

COMMUNICATING CHERISHMENT OF A CHILD

Special things I do	Special things I say	Special things I would like to say or do and why I have found them difficult to do.

Really what we say to each other is not nearly as important as how we say it. While these phrases can help us in communicating cherishing, one saying is often sufficient—"I love you." However, the way we say it can make a world of difference. Total engrossment through eye contact or through the physical expression while saying "I love you" can communicate meaning fully to the child.

Sometimes a child can get confused about an adult's love because of the necessity of discipline. On those days when everything seems to be going wrong, and, as a nurturer, you do not feel very comfortable about the interactions with a child, say something to clarify that your love is not affected by the child's actions and that his uniqueness is always cherished no matter what he does. One parent says: "No matter whatever happens or what you ever do, you can be sure of one thing . . . I'll always love you."

Relationship and Discipline Options for Behavior and Misbehavior

Billy comes running in from the yard crying hysterically. Bobby, his older brother, has hit him on the head with a rock. At the same time, Mom is at the door telling the Avon lady she doesn't have time to see her now because she is desperately behind in her housework, dinner is burning on the stove and the telephone is ringing.

As Billy comes in screaming Mom is tempted to tell him to shut up, or take a rock herself and throw it at Bobby, or resign as a parent. No matter what she does or doesn't do it will be wrong, according to some authority in adult-child relationships.

If Mom doesn't resign from parenthood and decides instead to turn off the stove, tell the caller to phone back and resist the temptation to act on impulse . . . what should she do? Some of the "experts" might answer:

Haim Ginott:[1] "Tell Bobby, people are not for hurting, if you must throw rocks, throw them at a tree."

Thomas Gordon:[2] "Let Billy know you have heard him and tell Bobby how you feel about what has happened."

Gerald Patterson:[3] "Either ignore the rock throwing or put Bobby in a time-out area. Save the attention for the times when Bobby is being nice to his brother."

Rudolph Dreikurs:[10] "Use logical consequences. If that doesn't work, try a mutual problem solving discussion with both children participating."

James Dobson:[11] "If you have instructed Bobby not to hurt his brother and he does it anyway, it is willful defiance. Spanking is the best thing for willful defiance."

Parents and teachers often face the dilemma of deciding on how to handle intense situations with children. Whatever the choice ultimately is, the adult often feels guilty because it may not have been the "right" choice according to one theory or another. What is lost in this process is the awareness that the "expert" is only a resource for ideas. The adult in the immediate situation

13

actually has a wide-range of options to choose from and is the final authority for deciding what is best.

There are many options or styles of relationships and discipline available to adults; most can probably be put into one of three categories: authoritarian, permissive, and "new styles." The new styles are discussed in Ginott's *Between Parent and Child,*[1] Thomas Gordon's *Parent Effectiveness Training,*[2] Gerald Patterson's *Living With Children,*[3] and Rudolph Dreikurs *Discipline Without Tears.*[10]

Ginott and Gordon emphasize dealing with feelings through listening, sending, and problem-solving techniques. Patterson describes behavior as something that is caused by the reactions of one person to another and he details how to increase and decrease certain behaviors by changing the adult's reactions to the child's behavior. (This method is frequently referred to as behavior modification.) Dreikurs describes four motives for misbehavior and the actions which are the most effective in dealing with each.

Many of the recent books on parent/child relationships have excellent ideas; however, each book suggests a different approach, and implies that its way is best. There is an on-going debate in the field of adult/child relationships about the best ways of relating to children. While healthy in some ways, the controversy often confuses the situation. Human relationships are such that there has never been and never will be any one "best way" for human beings to relate to each other. What is best for one situation or individual may not be best for another situation or individual.

Adults do not need to choose sides in the debate. It would be more helpful to look upon all the methods as offering possible alternatives. To be truly nurturing to another human being, one needs to become aware of all the options available, and the specific behaviors and situations appropriate to each option. Conceivably, an adult might utilize nine different relationship options, given nine different situations or behaviors. Adults need to choose options on the basis of what most comfortably fits the child, the nurturer, and the situation.

Most of the options available can be placed into nine categories:

ENFORCER—punishes, rewards, etc.

COMMANDER—orders, tells, etc.

INSTRUCTOR—uses logic, lectures, moralizes, etc.

ADVISER—sends solutions, prescribes, etc.

PREVENTER—arranges the environment or the situation so that the behavior will not occur.

CONFRONTER—confronts the child by stating the feeling being evoked by the behavior.

NEGOTIATOR—finds solutions through "give and take" discussions.

LISTENER—listens to the concerns of the child and helps find solutions.

RELINQUISHER—leaves decisions, solutions, etc. totally up to the child.

Without judging, consider all these to be viable options. Each is effective in some situations and ineffective in others. If an adult develops skills in all these areas, he or she will have alternatives for most situations involving parent-child or teacher-student relationships. The options in adult-child relationships can be placed on a scale ranging from autocratic (one who uses and keeps power) to abdicrat (one who gives up power).

RANGE OF NURTURING OPTIONS

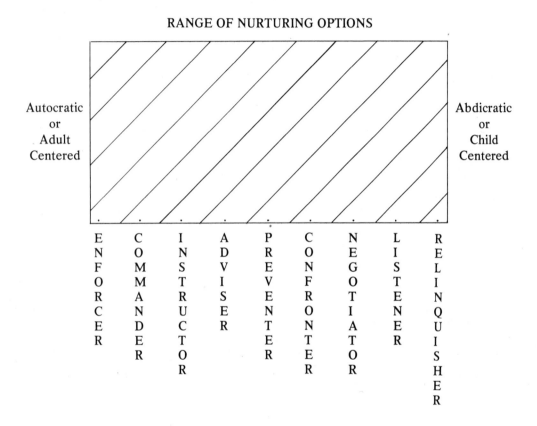

Autocratic or Adult Centered									Abdicratic or Child Centered
ENFORCER	COMMANDER	INSTRUCTOR	ADVISER	PREVENTER	CONFRONTATOR	NEGOTIATOR	LISTENER	RELINQUISHER

16

Exercise #1

On the form below, list one or two ways you implement each of the options, and what the child does that evokes this option.

Options	A couple of ways you use this option	Child's behavior that evokes this option
Enforcer		
Commander		
Instructor		
Adviser		
Preventer		
Confronter		
Negotiator		
Listener		
Relinquisher		

Exercise #2

Write one or two advantages and disadvantages to each option.

Option	Advantages	Disadvantages
Enforcer		
Commander		
Instructor		
Adviser		
Preventer		
Confronter		
Negotiator		
Listener		
Relinquisher		

While there is nothing inherently good or bad about each of the options or their placement on the range from autocrat to abdicrat, there are situations or behaviors for which one of the options may be more effective than another. For example:

Enforcer and Commander

When safety or physical harm is imminent—when a child runs from the yard or school grounds into the street without looking or when a couple of children are causing distraction in the family car or school bus as it is traveling down the freeway, etc.

Instructor

When the adult has information the child needs and doesn't have—when a boy is cutting with a knife in a manner that is likely to cause him to cut himself, etc.

Adviser

When the child definitely wants an answer to a situation he cannot resolve himself—when a girl comes home every day from school complaining that several children have been ganging up on her, etc.

Preventer

When a problem can be prevented by enriching or subduing a child's environment—removing fragile dishes from the reach of a toddler or by placing only safe play equipment on a school ground or in a backyard or by providing special areas or times for quietness and for loud active play at home and at school, etx.

Confronter

When a child can benefit from being aware of the feelings significant others have about something she or he is doing—when a child frequently interrupts telephone conversations, etc.

Negotiator

When there is an on-going conflict in a relationship—when two siblings are sharing a room and continually get into each other's way or when two children are constantly teasing each other at school, etc.

Listener

When a child is expressing strong feelings about something—when a boy is talking about feeling left out of the in-group of boys at school or in the neighborhood, etc.

Relinquisher

When the child is capable of, and can profit by, finding his own solution to a problem—when a child is working on a difficult model and is having difficulty but wants to continue to do it alone, etc.

There are many more examples for each option that will be explored later, but the most important thing to consider is not the way that things are listed in categories above but the way things are working for you in your relationship with children.

Exercise #3

Look at what you have listed in Exercise #1, and think about how the options fit the behaviors. For the options that do not fit, what do you think would work better for you and your child? Write in the third column to the right either: "It's working" or list the name of the option that you think would be more effective.

It can often be difficult to decide which option to use when a behavior occurs. It can be helpful to realize which type of behavior is happening before deciding which option to use. There are four major types of behavior:

Enjoyable
The behavior of a child which evokes positive adult feelings.

Intolerable
The behavior of a child that the adult feels must stop immediately.

Tolerable
The behavior of a child that needs to change but can be endured for the moment.

Concernable
The behavior of a child that causes the adult to want to help.

Behavior Categories	Examples of Behavior
Enjoyable	Helping each other. Playing cooperatively. Hugging you.
Intolerable	Older child beating up younger child. Non-swimmer running dangerously close to edge of a swimming pool.
Tolerable	Taking too long a time to get dressed in the morning. Two children frequently putting each other down.
Concernable	Having nightmares. Looking upset. Crying.

Some behaviors fit into different categories depending on the tolerance level of the adult. For instance, some adults have a very difficult time tolerating crying. Therefore for a specific individual, crying might be categorized under intolerable behavior rather than concernable behavior. An adult's level of tolerance for certain behaviors can have a direct effect on one's ability to nurture. (How to deal with, and sometimes change, your own tolerance will be discussed later.)

Also, one's tolerance can change considerably from day to day and moment to moment, depending on the situation, moods, and other people who are present. For example, a child playing with a toy dump truck in the sand pile could quite often be categorized as an enjoyable behavior. However, the exact behavior in a changed situation could possibly become intolerable; for example, if the child fills the dump truck with sand and then carries it into the middle of the livingroom and begins dumping sand in piles on the rug. It might be enjoyable to wake up to the "pitter-patter of little feet" running through the house; however, if you have been up quite late the night before socializing and have an intense headache upon awaking, this behavior could switch from enjoyable to intolerable. Sloppy table manners might at times be tolerable but not when company comes (particularly grandma and grandpa).

Exercise #4
On a piece of paper describe as many behaviors as you can think of for a specific child. At the end of a few minutes, turn to the Behavior Categories Worksheet on the next page. Under column #1 place each of the behaviors next to the category that you feel best fits the behavior.

BEHAVIOR CATEGORIES WORKSHEET

Behavior Categories	1 Examples of one of my children's (or student's) behavior	2	3	4
Enjoyable				
Intolerable				
Tolerable				
Concernable				

After you have finished Exercise #4, review the categories of behavior. Are there any behaviors for which you would like to change your level of tolerability? Are there some tolerable behaviors you would like to enjoy, or are there some intolerable behaviors you would like to tolerate?

Exercise #5

Label column #2 on the Behavior Categories Worksheet "What I do." Briefly describe what you do when each behavior in column #1 occurs.

Exercise #6

Label column #3 "Name of the Option." Put the name of the option that fits each description listed in Exercise #5 (Enforcer, Commander, Instructor, Adviser, Preventer, Confronter, Negotiator, Listener, Relinquisher).

Exercise #7

Label column #4 "Which Option Would be Best." Beside each option that you listed under #3, put the word "same" if you feel it is best for you to use in the situation. If you do not think it was the best one to use, put the name of a better option.

As mentioned earlier, all the nurturing options are viable for specific behavior in specific situations. However, depending upon one's own personal style, some options fit certain categories of behavior more effectively than others. Here are a few illustrations:

Behavior Category	Options	Examples
Enjoyable	Listener	Letting a child know you really enjoy what he or she is saying by intensive listening.
	Relinquisher	Letting a child fully enjoy an experience by not intruding in it.
	Enforcer	Giving positive attention to enjoyable behavior to increase its frequency.
Intolerable	Preventer	Providing active and quiet areas and/or times within your home or classroom.
	Enforcer	Implementing consequences for behavior.
	Commander	Telling a child to stop doing or to start doing something.
Tolerable	Negotiator	"Talking out" a conflict with two or more people involved.
	Confronter	Telling a child the feelings evoked by a behavior.
	Adviser	Suggesting some alternatives for resolving a conflict or a problem.
	Instructor	Reasoning with a child about his or her behavior.
Concernable	Listener	Without judging, let the child know you hear his or her feelings.
	Relinquisher	Letting a child struggle through a problem on his own so that he can learn through natural consequences and/or trial and error, etc.
	Adviser	Suggesting ways that a child can resolve feelings, or ways he or she can resolve the problem.
	Instructor	Telling a child what should be done about the problem or what should be done about his or her feelings.

Effective Options for Intolerable and Enjoyable Behavior

Freedom is one of the most precious gifts of life and bondage is enslavement by the consequences of immature impulses. Children who must wait for life's experiences to teach them the consequences of aversive or destructive behavior often form impulse habits which inhibit maturing and limit severely the choices they can make in life. Adults who help the child realize the consequences of behavior in a more immediate way than nature can provide may actually be increasing the child's chances of becoming a freely functioning human being.

Intolerable behavior is any child's behavior that the adult feels must stop immediately. There is a very thin line between intolerable behavior and tolerable behavior. Each adult because of her or his background of experiences might draw the line at a different spot. Whether the adult has a few types of behaviors that are under the intolerable line or many, two types are usually always there:

1. any action which is likely to cause serious injury to the child or other people.
2. any action which results in the destruction of other's possessions or property.

The following examples might or might not be intolerable, depending upon the level of tolerability of the adult:

(1) Johnny is the classroom clown. Every time he falls off his chair, stumbles over someone's foot, or drops a book, his classmates laugh at him. Because these actions have become more and more frequent, the teacher and students have found it impossible to accomplish daily tasks. Johnny's teacher has lectured to him several times about his behavior, but the few times that he has made an effort to stop joking around, people do not react, so the incidences of clowning continue to increase. Why?

(2) Wendy is happily babbling in her crib, and her mother breathes a

sigh of relief because she can finally get to that pile of laundry. But before long, Wendy is crying in a tantrum-like manner and throwing the toys from her crib all over the room. As her mother runs into the room anxiously looking for a way to calm her, Wendy's screams intensify. Mother finally holds the baby warmly and rocks her, and the crying subsides for the moment. However, after a few days of this pattern, Wendy happily babbles less and tantrums more. Why?

(3) Bill and Bobby are constructively playing a game together. Dad takes this opportunity to sit down and read the paper without interruption. Just about the time he has finished the first paragraph, he finds it impossible to concentrate because the game has deteriorated into a fight. Dad yells at them to stop. When they don't, he spanks both of them and lectures them about hitting and screaming at each other. As time goes on, the boys seldom play constructively and seem to be constantly fighting. Why?

Much of a child's behavior is modeled after the significant others in his or her environment. Behavior, for the most part, gets its nourishment from personal satisfaction (including power-seeking and revenge) and attention. The intensity and frequency of the attention given can be closely related to the increase and decrease of a type of behavior.*

If you want a behavior to increase, pay attention to it. If you want a behavior to decrease, ignore it, or use an action that has the least amount of interaction or attention involved.

Nurturers want to see enjoyable behavior increase and intolerable behavior decrease; unfortunately, providing nourishment does not come naturally. The natural thing to do is to give intense attention when all hell is breaking loose and try to find a quiet part in the day for oneself when things are going well.

When a nurturer is busy, tired, or both (which adults often are because of the responsibilities of nurturing), there is a natural tendency not to notice enjoyable behavior and to feel relieved from involvement with the child for the moment.

Human beings, especially children, thrive from attention. When positive attention is not frequently available, any kind of attention will do, even if it results in pain or discomfort.

---

*This is also sometimes true with behavior that is caused by physiological problems, i.e. diet deficiencies, developmental lags, neurological problems, temporary illnesses, etc. However, the advice of a medical specialist might be combined with the methods in this chapter, if physical problems are suspected.

Exercise #1

For a specific child, list intolerable behaviors.	List what you usually do when these behaviors occur. (Briefly describe your reaction or lack of reaction to each behavior.)
For the same child, list enjoyable behaviors.	

If you are a normal nurturer, you will probably notice that the intolerable behaviors listed in Exercise #1 receive more of your undivided attention than do the enjoyable behaviors. While the nurturing process can be enhanced by reversing attention patterns, desire and willpower on the part of the nurturer often is not enough to bring about this change. A practical process for changing adult attention patterns has been developed and is successful in both school and home situations. The process has three main elements in it:

1. Preventing—If the opportunity for the intolerable behavior can be removed from the environment without undesirable side effects, remove it.
2. Selective Attention—If the opportunity should not or cannot be removed, ignore the behavior (most intolerable behaviors are very difficult to ignore unless a "time-out" procedure is used). Give give attention to the enjoyable behavior instead.
3. Nurturing Consequences—When the behavior cannot be ignored, use

a nurturing consequence. Nurturing consequences also are often effective with behavior that is motivated by power-seeking or revenge.

CAUTION: Be sure the behavior you expect is something that is within the ability and age level of the child.

Preventing: Removing the Opportunity or Temptation from the Environment.

Dodson in *How to Parent*[12] provides the following illustration:

> Suppose you visited a nursery school or kindergarten and found the room stripped down with no educational or play equipment whatsoever. No blocks, no trucks, cars, wagons, crayons, paint, paper, clay—nothing for the children to play with. When you went out on the playground you observed the same things: no climbing equipment, no slides, large hollow blocks, tricycles or wagons. If a teacher actually tried to teach some youngsters in such a barren or unstimulating environment, he or she would have his or her hands full of discipline problems.
>
> Look at your own house and backyard. Is this one which has little in the way of play equipment? Is it full of adult things that a child must not touch? If so, you probably have a number of needless discipline problems on your hands. But if you provide an interesting and stimulating environment in your home or backyard, you will be using environment control to prevent discipline problems.
>
> Think of long vacation trips in a car with small youngsters. There are some parents to whom such trips are nightmares simply because they provide nothing for young children to do during such a long trip. They don't take along games or art materials or surprises to introduce when the sibling rivalry gets sticky. They don't plan where their children can get out and run around for a hit. Then the parents wonder why the youngsters are fighting, whining, and making the trip miserable. An ounce of environmental control for such a long trip is worth a pound of discipline after the trouble starts.

The more adequately the nurturer can arrange the environment for the child, the fewer intolerable problems will arise.

Gordon[2] in the chapter, "Changing the Unacceptable Behavior by Changing the Environment," in *Parent Effectiveness Training*, suggests that the following can be done to remove opportunities, temptations, or conflicts from the environment:

1. enrich the environment
2. impoverish it
3. simplify it
4. restrict it
5. child-proof it
6. substitute one activity for another
7. prepare the child for changes
8. plan ahead with older children

The nursery school example in Dodson's quote above is an illustration of the importance of enriched environments; sometimes, however, the environment *needs* to be improverished if there are too many things stimulating the child. For example, just before bedtime children often need a chance to calm down. Simplifying the environment means providing activities that are at a child's current level and stage of development. Examples are: buying clothes that are easy for the child to put on, building a stool or box so a child can reach things in his closet, etc. Child-proofing the environment basically means keeping fragile or dangerous things out of reach of young children. Problems sometimes can be avoided by substituting one activity for another; for instance, if a child likes to throw things and frequently throws rocks at people, direct him or her to throw a ball at a target or play catch.

Exercise #2

Return to Exercise #1 and locate the intolerable behaviors that you feel could be reduced by changing the environment. Make a specific commitment to yourself for each change in the environment that could be implemented within your home or classroom.

Selective Attention

As mentioned earlier, most intolerable behavior needs to be corrected immediately and therefore is not conducive to the technique of ignoring and waiting for behavior to change. However, there may be some intolerable behaviors where the immediacy of change can wait for a few moments. In these situations, the effectiveness of ignoring is greatly determined by being aware of, and reacting to enjoyable behavior that should be happening in place of the intolerable behavior.

Example: Shirley, a fifth-grade student, frequently interrupted others in her classroom, whether it was the teacher explaining something to another child, or to the class, or to a group of children working together on a project, Shirley would often blurt out a question or comment without waiting for the appropriate time. At first her teacher responded by telling her to be quiet; however, the intolerable behavior increased. Finally, Shirley's teacher decided to ignore the behavior and give attention to other children who were waiting their turn.

The teacher instructed the other members of the classroom not to react to Shirley when she interrupted. The next time Shirley interrupted, there was no reaction, comment or punishment. She tried several times again and still received no reaction. When she waited to ask a question or to make a comment in the appropriate manner without interrupting others, the teacher responded to her immediately answering her question, talking with her about her idea, and indicating appreciation for her appropriate way of talking in the classroom. Within a few days her behavior pattern changed positively.

The most important element that existed in the situation described above was the way enjoyable behavior began to work for Shirley and how intolerable behavior stopped working for her. Ignoring intolerable behavior will often be

yes!

ineffective unless the enjoyable behavior that should replace it is shown appreciation by the nurturer.

Another way to avoid giving attention to intolerable behavior is to use a "time-out" procedure. The more intense intolerable behaviors often cannot be ignored unless the offender is removed from the situation. A specific chair, space, or room could be designated the time-out area. The main elements of time-out should be:

1. not overdone (5-10 minutes is enough depending upon the age).
2. far enough away from others that attention is cut-off.
3. close enough to the adult that it is supervised.
4. enforced—the child gets the message that he or she must stay in the time-out area for the allotted time.

Example: Seven-year-old Jenny frequently hit and pushed her four-year-old brother to monopolize the toys in the yard. Dad decided to use a combination of time-out for the intolerable behavior and attention and privileges for the desired behavior that he wanted in its place (i.e., Jenny cooperatively sharing and taking turns with the toys). He informed Jenny that if she tried to take the toys through physical force he would have her sit in a time-out chair for five minutes to "cool off" and think over how she should behave. He also told her that on any day she didn't need any time-outs, she would have the privilege of the backyard toys for herself for a half-hour before dinner.

The next time Jenny knocked down her brother to get a toy, she was told to go to the time-out chair. She refused to go to the time-out chair, so Dad, without any further words, firmly picked her up and placed her in the time-out chair. He set the timer for five minutes. After 30 seconds Jenny was out of the chair. Dad put her back in the chair and started the timer back five minutes again. After a couple of more tries, Jenny discovered that the only way she would be able to get out of the chair was to stay for the five minutes. (Most children will test the limits the adult sets. Putting extra, sometimes exasperating, effort at this crucial point will usually save considerable time and energy in the long run.)

When the timer bell rang, Dad came over to the time-out chair and asked, "What did you do that caused you to be in the time-out chair?" and "What can you do so that you won't wind up back there?" Jenny refused to answer. Dad said, "OK, you stay and I will check back with you in a minute or so to see if you have an answer." When Dad returned, Jenny answered the questions and returned to play in the yard. She shared and took turns with her brother several times during the next hour. Dad made a point to show Jenny a couple of times his appreciation for the way she was behaving. Within a week Jenny was frequently earning her privilege, and within a couple of weeks her new behavior was working so well that she no longer needed appreciation for reinforcement.

Exercise #3

Return to Exercise #1 and see if there are any behaviors listed that could possibly be ignored (including ignoring through a time-out procedure). If there are some, for the next week or so keep a small index card or piece of paper with you and mark each time you successfully ignore the intolerable behavior and give attention to the enjoyable behavior that could replace it. Keeping track of this will help to increase consistency. Consistency in ignoring is essential because if you ignore a behavior ten times but respond to it on the 11th, the last response can undo the efforts of all the previous ones.

Nurturing Consequences

Nurturing consequences help a child learn that there are no free tickets to life. What everyone chooses to do, there is always a Piper to pay. The price of real freedom is usually responsibility. Nurturing consequences help the adult take action in a constructive, character-building way that in turn helps the child become responsible for his or her actions. The consequences are intended to be very similar to what naturally happens in life. The main difference is that the consequence happens quicker and at an earlier stage than what might naturally happen. This increases the possibility that learning can take place before disaster occurs.

A nurturing consequence would have most of the following elements:

1. *Familiar*
   The child knows that the consequence will be consistently used for a specific situation.

2. *Fitting*
   The consequence fits the situation—is as close to a natural extension of what the child did as is practical.

3. *Fair*
   The consequence is not overdone to the point where it loses its meaningfulness related to the offense. A child seldom receives more than one consequence for one incidence of intolerable behavior. The consequence fits the age level of the child.

4. *Fast*
   The nurturer uses action rather than words as the main emphasis of the consequence. The consequence is implemented immediately after the behavior occurs. The consequence is short enough to allow an opportunity for correcting the behavior following the consequence within the situation that occurred.

5. *Firm*
   The consequence is implemented with sureness and consistency.

6. *Focused*
   The consequence is focused on the behavior or action that is occurring —not on the personality or character of the child.

Familiar

Children frequently will respond more readily to a consequence that they anticipate. Using the same consequence (if it is effective) each time a certain type of behavior occurs enhances security for the child and consistency for the adult.

If the child knows that a specific consequence is about to occur, he or she has the opportunity to correct the behavior before the consequence is implemented sometimes removing the necessity for it. Krumboltz[13] uses the term "cuing" to describe this technique in the following example:

> At the beginning of a race the starter will say, "On your mark, get set, go." The word "go" is the cue for the runners to begin running. The words "on your mark" and "get set" are anticipatory cues to prepare the runners for the signal to go. At times it is important for the children to react promptly when a cue is given. Anticipatory cues serve to alert them that when the final cue is given, they must move quickly.

Some specific cuing comments could be:

"In five minutes, it will be your bedtime. Be ready to go to bed as soon as this TV program is over."

"In three minutes it will be time to get out of the swimming pool. Be sure to do all you want to do in the next three minutes so you will get out immediately when I tell you to."

"By the time I count to five, you should . . ."

Children, particularly younger children, have a very difficult time detaching themselves from a specific activity in which they are involved. Cuing the child can give him or her the chance to gradually get uninvolved with the immediate activity so that the next behavior can be initiated.

Sometimes it is also helpful to have an element of motivation included in a request for a child to behave in a certain way. This particularly applies to situations where something has to be done immediately, such as a child having to get ready quickly because you are on the brink of being late to an appointment.

Homme[14] uses the term "First-Then" to describe this process. First specify the behavior expected, i.e., "Pick up the toys and put them away" and then provide the motivator, "then you may go outside to play with your friends." Another example would be, "First get dressed and make your bed" and "then you may have breakfast." This approach provides motivation for having something done immediately that needs to be done, but will work consistently only if the "then" is not made available to the child until he or she does the "first."

Fitting

Making a consequence "fitting" to the behavior can increase its effectiveness and meaningfulness. The most fitting types of consequences are "natural" consequences. An example of a natural consequence is when a child touches a burner on a hot stove, he or she feels the pain and learns not to touch it again. While a nurturer might strive to have consequences be natural, it is often impractical to wait because of safety and time factors. However, keeping in mind the natural consequences of specific behaviors can help to fit the consequence as close to natural as possible. Here are some examples:

1. Clean up mess created.
2. Repair damage done.
3. Work for money to replace damage.
4. Make amends.
5. Do something nice for the person offended.
6. Temporarily lose the right to participate in an activity in which the intolerable behavior occurred, e.g., if the intolerable behavior occurred in the backyard or on the playground, the child is removed from that area for a short period of time—usually five minutes is enough.
7. Making up the time misused (if a child will not settle down at bedtime, the next evening he goes to bed a minute early for each minute he wasted at bedtime, etc.)

CAUTION: Aversive conditions, if too intense or powerful, may promote fears that will persist long after the actual danger has passed.[13] For instance, if a child is a little too reckless around swimming pools or at the beach, a healthy respect for the water can be taught without hysterical references to the dangers of drowning.

Fair and Fast

The intensity or aversiveness of a consequence can be affected by its fairness. A consequence which may not be too aversive, such as picking up all the tanbark a child has thrown out of a play area, could become quite aversive if it were exaggerated over too long a period of time by making a child pick up tanbark and replace it during all his free time for several days. Most consequences can be fair if the child is asked to undo what he or she has done and the time element involved is not delayed or excessive, i.e., usually immediately, lasting somewhere between five and ten minutes.

Having a relatively brief time element also increases the opportunity for the child to initiate the enjoyable behavior that should replace the intolerable behavior. For instance, if a child has been removed from the situation for fighting with other children, after he or she has had five to ten minutes to cool down and think it over, the child should be allowed to return to the situation so he or she can try to interact with those same children on a constructive basis. Learning this immediately, rather than not having the opportunity until the next day or the next week, can greatly increase the chances of the enjoyable behavior replacing the intolerable behavior.

Firm

Before implementing a consequence, be sure you are comfortable with the decision that the behavior needs a consequence. Once you have assured yourself that the decision is appropriate, act without hesitance. In this kind of a situation negotiation before completion of a consequence could mislead the child into believing you can be talked out of the consequence. Save nurturing consequences for those behaviors that are so intensive that there is no time for mutual problem solving. Then, when you do choose to use negotiating (either following the completion of a consequence or with behaviors that do not require immediate consequences), the mutual problem solving can be an authentic give-and-take discussion between adult and child.

Focused

If the child needs to be reasoned with about behavior because he or she might not understand the implications of the situation, the reasoning is usually far more effective following the consequence because the child usually is more calm and able to listen. At the moment of the intolerable behavior, actually removing the child from the situation or having the child correct the situation is often more effective than moralizing.

If words are necessary, they should be directed at the behavior and what can immediately be done to correct the behavior. It is quite important to avoid any comments which might label the character or personality of the child, i.e., "You are to stop hitting him immediately" as opposed to "You are a bad boy." It is usually much easier to enforce a consequence when you do not arouse another individual's defenses. Besides, most people derive perceptions of who they are from the significant others in their environment. If a child is told often enough that he is a "bad boy," he will become one.

Nurturing consequences are important to the nurturer as well as to the child. Patterson[3] indicates that observation of people in social settings how that the individual who gives the most reinforcement receives the most reinforcement. Additionally, one usually receives the same kind of consequences that he or she uses.

In other words— *you get what you give.*[3]

A nurturer who is not fair with a child usually finds the child to be frequently unfair in reacting back to the nurturer and others.

There are several sayings that can be used to remind yourself or a child of the nature of nurturing consequences:

1. You can be as free as you can be responsible.
2. Your freedom stops when it violates the freedom of others.
3. Abuse it and you lose it (things, time, freedom).
4. If you break it, fix it.
5. What you do is what you get or what you earn is what you get.

Exercise #4

For each of the following examples of behavior, jot down the nurturing consequence you might use (for the sake of practice assume you would be comfortable with the decision that each of these behaviors needs a consequence).

Example: A four-year-old child who frequently rides her Big Wheel into the street.

Example: A 14-year-old who throws rocks at the neighbor's house and breaks the window.

Example: A seven-year-old who was told to come straight home from school but instead went to the neighborhood store first and stole some candy.

Example: A nine-year-old who frequently starts fights on the playground or in the neighborhood.

Example: A 12-year-old who on field trips or family outings will not stay with the others; instead he or she frequently gets into dangerous situations like running close to the edge of a steep cliff.

Since nurturing consequences are tailored to meet a unique situation, there is no "right" answer to each of the examples in Exercise #4. Therefore, the following opinions of the author should be considered only one of many ways the situations could be handled.

Example: A four-year-old child who frequently rides her Big Wheel into the street.

Immediately remove the child from the Big Wheel. Impound the Big Wheel in the garage for five minutes. Get a commitment from the child about staying on the sidewalk just before unimpounding the vehicle. Repeat this, increasing the length of the impounding time if needed.

Example: A 14-year-old who throws rocks at the neighbor's house and breaks the window.

Instruct him or her to talk with the neighbor about the window—with parental help if needed. The window could be replaced by the child working for the neighbor or parent for the number of hours that would equal the number of dollars the window cost.

Example: A seven-year-old who was told to come straight home from school but instead went to the neighborhood store first and stole some candy.

Take the child to the store and have him or her talk to the store manager about the theft. The candy is to be returned or paid for. The privilege of walking home from school is revoked for a day and the parent accompanies the child home from school. If the problem repeats itself, the privilege of walking home unsupervised may have to be revoked for a longer period of time.

Example: A nine-year-old who frequently starts fights on the playground or in the neighborhood.

Have the child talk with his or her "partner in pugilism" for the purpose of making a "plan for peace." The two must come to a mutual agreement before the child is allowed to once again play.

Example: A 12-year-old who on field trips or family outings will not stay with the others; instead he or she frequently gets into dangerous situations like running close to the edge of a steep cliff.

Remove the child from the edge of the cliff. Have him or her lose the freedom of walking around for five minutes. At the end of five minutes get a commitment from the child about staying with the group. If the child continues to stray away from the family or group, he or she should lose the privilege of participating in the rest of the present trip or all of the next one.

Exercise #5

Return to Exercise #1 and look at the intolerable behaviors listed. Determine which would be best dealt with through nurturing consequences. Look at the consequences or reactions that are listed on the right side of the page. Are they nurturing? If not, list those that you think could be nurturing for that specific behavior.

The main goals of parenthood and teaching are to nurture an individual into becoming a person who:
1. feels good about himself or herself.
2. can handle responsibility.
3. can relate positively to others.
4. can be a positive contributor to society.

Immediate consequences are often a necessary, temporary discomfort imposed for the purpose of preventing a child's intolerable impulses from inhibiting progress toward these main goals.

According to Dodson,[12]:

> Consequences imposed by adults are necessary only to the degree that self-regulation does not exist in a child. The word discipline means to instruct, educate or train. The word discipline is related to the word disciple. When you discipline a child, you may be really training him to be a disciple of you.

Decisions about reacting to a behavior, whether it be tolerable or intolerable, might be helped by the following quote from the excellent book, *I See a Child*, by Cindy Herbert,[15]:

The Monster

You're afraid of me!
I throw things.
I hit people.
You prefer not to see.
I talk back and you do nothing.
You never tell me what I should or shouldn't do,
Except in a most polite way.
You're afraid of me
And I'm scared.
Who knows what you might let me do?
Please, please tell me when to stop—
Don't be afraid of me!

Effective Options for Concernable Behavior

Nine-year-old Danny's dog has just been hit by a car. He and his pet have been inseparable. Spot went with him on his paper route, hiked with him in the hills nearby, and slept at the foot of his bed at night. They have been constant companions and now they may be parted forever. Danny is mad at himself for not having Spot stay closer when they crossed the street. Profoundly sad and frightened at the potential loneliness, he turns to his parents with tears in his eyes, screaming, "Spot can't die—he can't, he can't!"

Concernable behavior causes the adult to want to help a child who is having strong feelings about something or is upset about a problem. The child usually communicates his distress through words, voice tone, behavior, and body language (body posture, facial expression, eye expression, etc.)

The words the child uses often give clues to the adult for a starting point in helping the child cope more effectively with his or her problem. In concernable behavior, though the nurturer might be concerned, worried, or anxious about the problem, it is the child that has the more intense feelings. The child might indicate concernable problems by making statements like:

"Nobody will play with me."

"I'm lonely."

"I can't do anything right."

"I'm the ugliest girl in my class."

"I really miss daddy."

"This darn homework."

"Everybody picks on me."

"I'm sick and tired of being called fatso."

"Nobody likes me."

Exercise #1

In the space provided below, to the list of examples on page 00, add a couple of things you have heard a child say that indicates concernable problems. Beside each one of the previous quotes, including the ones you have added, write a hypothetical one-sentence response.

Which options did you use in responding to the child in Exercise #1? If your response was a question, which option would you have used after getting an answer? Most adults use the following options when a child expresses a concernable problem:

Adviser - "If I were you, I'd ignore the kids who call you fatso."
"Try to forget about Spot, it just hurts to think about him."

Instructor - "If you want someone to play with, do this . . ."
"Next time you take a dog for a walk, use a leash and looks both ways."

Commander - "Stop complaining about your homework and do it!"

Giving advice or instruction can sometimes be helpful and realistic—especially when the child needs a quick answer or solution to an immediate problem. However, for a solution to last, it is often necessary to first deal with the feelings that underline the problem. Unexpressed aversive human feelings have a tendency to accumulate in a person. One feeling builds on top of another until we are brimming over and the feelings spill out in uncontrollable ways (temper tantrums, physical violence, etc.) or they stay inside and put pressure on the mind (depression, etc.) or the body (stomach ulcers, high blood pressure, heart attack, etc.)

Uncontrollable outbursts or internal damage to one's health through repressing feelings can be prevented by getting the feelings out through verbalization or non-destructive physical action. The problem with initially advising or instructing is that it sometimes denies the opportunity to get feelings out.

When concernable behavior occurs, listen without judgment before considering solutions or advice.

When, through listening, it is determined the problem is one the child can handle on his or her own, the Relinquisher option might be used instead of Adviser or Instructor. The Preventer option might also sometimes be an effective follow-up (or predecessor) to the Listener option. Emotions can sometimes be soothed by changing things in the environment that cause them.

Below are some examples of implementing the Preventer option for concernable behavior:

Example #1: Five-year-old Billy often feels inferior and left out. His eight-year-old brother, John, has lots of friends on the block to play with. Billy wants to play with John and his friends because he doesn't have any friends his own age. John and his friends exclude Billy because he is too young. When they do give in and let him come along, he always gets frustrated because he is not physically or emotionally ready for their activities.

If you were a parent and heard Billy's daily tears and expressions of loneliness, how would you implement the Preventer option to deal with this behavior?

Billy's parents located the nearest five-year-olds in the neighborhood. Since none of them lived on the same block, his parents arranged with other parents a method of supervising children as they walked to each other's homes. At first Billy's parents arranged some special activities for him and his friends, but it wasn't long before informal play was enough to keep the bonds of friendship going.

Example #2: Jennifer is in a second grade school room which uses the learning center approach. There are several centers in the room for specific subject areas, such as reading, math, and art. The students are allowed to move freely from center to center as long as none gets overcrowded. Most of the students are responding positively to this approach, but not Jennifer. She spends most of her time by herself either daydreaming or resting her head in her arms quietly weeping. Since Jennifer's learning readiness level is not as developed as most of her classmates, she needs another year of pre-reading and pre-math skills development.

If you were Jennifer's teacher, how would you implement the Preventer option to deal with this concernable behavior?

Jennifer's teacher first tried to provide some separate work at her own level by placing visual motor perceptual worksheets and numbers awareness activities at the various learning centers. Since these activities require oral directions, volunteer helpers (adults and older students) were provided as often as possible. This approach would have worked for many children but it didn't for Jennifer. She was very self-conscious about the fact that her individualized work was much lower than that of the other students and her reaction was further withdrawal and more intense weeping.

What would you have done if you still felt a Preventer option would be the most effective?

Jennifer's teacher placed her in another classroom where there were many children like Jennifer. Jennifer's new teacher worked with her group in a very structured way, with step-by-step instructions, frequent positive reinforcement, and no chance to fail.

Example #3: As mentioned in Chapter 1, Armondo is a very capable student who tries too hard. He gets so nervous when there is a test he often misreads the questions making several mistakes. He feels the single reason he is accepted by others is because he is "smart."

What would you do if you decided to use the Preventer option for this situation?

For long range effectiveness, Armondo's parents and teacher agreed to place as much emphasis as possible on communicating to Armondo that he is "cherished" more for his uniqueness than for his achievement. For immediate effects, Armondo was provided with special essay examinations when tests needed to be given. He was allowed to write down both his knowledge and opinions about the subject, and was given as much time as he needed to complete the examination.

Preventing can also be somewhat mixed with listening. If a child feels heard, a solution often becomes unnecessary or the child becomes capable of determining the solution through clearer self-understanding.

One of the quickest ways to relieve intense feelings is to communicate them to another human being who cares.

It is very difficult to make a decision about a problem while undergoing intense anguish; decisions need to be saved for calmer moments.

Listening to an upset human being requires skill and patience. There is a natural tendency to ask a lot of questions rather than listen, which may be perceived as threatening or may have a tendency to lead the individual away from his feelings.

If you have a question to ask—listen first. In the end, the question may be answered without asking.

The following exercises will provide experiences in methods of listening that do not require questioning. Each separate exercise may seem to be an incomplete form of communication. However, when you synthesize all the exercises they will provide the opportunity to experience one of the most caring forms of human communication.

Exercise #2

Ask a partner to talk with you about a child—describing the child and the joys and sorrows, ups and downs of the child's life experiences. Your task is to listen intently with total engrossment. However, when you respond you are not to question, suggest, or judge. The only thing you are to say is "um-hmmm."

After a few minutes reverse roles; you talk about a child with your partner listening and responding with "um-hmmm."

At the end of a few minutes discuss: How does it feel to be listened to in this manner? Was it difficult not to question, suggest or judge? Was just saying "um-hmm" too limited?

Exercise #3

Ask a partner to talk with you about a pet peeve or something that really concerns him or her. If it is difficult to think of something in those areas, talk about a specific child who is having a problem or talk about one's agreements and disagreements with this chapter or this book. After five minutes switch roles. You become the talker and the partner becomes the listener. Again you are not to question, suggest or judge. This time you are to imagine you are a human tape recorder. When you have a chance to respond, do so by only saying what (or part of what) you have heard your partner say. The difference between you and a real tape recorder is that you can paraphrase what has been said and express it with feeling and engrossment.

At the end of the exercise discuss: How did it feel to be listened to in this manner? As a listener, was it difficult not to question, suggest, or judge? Were paraphrasing tape recorder responses too limited?

The listening techniques experienced in the last two exercises are helpful in avoiding the natural tendency to question, suggest, and judge. However, more is usually needed than just "um-hmm" and paraphrasing to make the communication meaningful.

When an individual is hurting, he or she needs a way of getting pain from the inside to the outside. Upset feelings are painful but difficult to get out. A person can talk to himself or herself all day and can never clearly "see" what is being said—and felt. A caring friend, parent, or teacher can become an "emotional mirror" through which an individual can more clearly see and understand his own feelings. Clearer "vision" and understanding helps relieve the intensity of unpleasant feelings (though at first they may temporarily escalate before diminishing).

Communication through which this can be done is called either reflective listening[1] or active listening.[2] It is a form of listening and responding that focuses on feelings, emulates engrossment, and is nonjudgmentally empathic. We will refer to this form of communication as ARE Listening. (A = active, R = reflective, E = empathic and engrossed) as in "ARE you listening?" The main task of the ARE Listener is to separate feelings from content and let the individual know his or her feelings have been heard. The paraphrasing response reflected the content of what was being said. For example, if a teenage boy was talking to a friend about asking a girl out for his first date, he might have said something like:

"I keep thinking today is the day I'll ask her to the party . . . and then when I see her, I choke up and split."

Reflecting the content of this statement could be:

"Each day you think you'll ask her but when you see her, you back out of it."

To reflect the feelings of communication, one needs to:

1. determine the feelings that underlie the statement,
2. determine the words or sentence to reflect the feelings.

What feeling or feelings might underlie the teenager's statement? Worry? Fear? Anxiousness? Embarrassment? Nervousness? Though you are never sure of another's exact feelings, reflecting your assumptions of feelings can help the individual internally clarify feelings.

How could one of the feelings you assume the teenager had be reflected in words or a sentence? First, decide which feeling seems to you to best fit

44

what the person is expressing. If you were to decide "fear," you could reflect it in one of the following ways:

"When you see her, the fear of her saying 'no' makes you uptight," or,
"You're afraid you'll make a fool out of yourself," or,
"You're afraid she'll turn you down," or,
"It's a scary situation," or,
"Kind of scary."

The way the ARE Listener responds is more important than the words that are said.

The core of ARE Listening is the communication of caring and empathy.

The important thing is that you care enough to listen and try. If you are not right on target with the exact feeling, ARE Listening leaves the door open for the individual to correct you and you can reflect the correction. Example:

"You are afraid she'll turn you down."
"No, I'm not afraid of that. It's just that I don't know if I can come up with the right words."
"You're worried about how you're going to say it."
"Yeah, like the words might come out all mixed up."

Exercise #4

Look again at Exercise #1—
    a. List a feeling or two for each of the child's statements.
    b. Determine the phrase or sentence for reflecting these feelings.
    c. Compare these ARE Listening statements with those in Exercise #1.

Child Statement	The Underlying Feeling	ARE Listening Statement

ARE Listening can be single statements or a flow of conversation depending on the situation and the individual's need to talk at that moment. The following is an example of a father (F) ARE Listening to his nine-year-old son's (S) feelings about a friend who is quite competitive:

S: "I hate Joe!"

F: "You are angry with Joe."

S: "No, I HATE him!!"

F: "You hate Joe."

S: "All he does is push me around."

F: "His pushing makes you mad."

S: "Yeah! I'm going to kill him!"

F: "You really want to get even with him."

S: "I'm going down there and punch him in the nose."

F: "He really upsets you."

S: "He always cheats in games."

F: "It doesn't seem fair to you."

S: "Yeah! What he says, goes. When I call a foul he just shouts me down."

F: "It really bugs you."

S: "And when I make a mistake like dropping a pass—he calls me 'spaz' and things like that."

F: "You feel put down by him."

S: "And then everybody joins in the teasing."

F: "It's like everybody gets down on you."

S: "Yeah. And all because of Joe. I'm going to kill him . . . tomorrow."

(The voice tone and body posture are far more relaxed and less intense than they were at the beginning of the conversation.)

The above example illustrates the combined use of ARE Listening and occasional tape recorder paraphrasing. In this specific case the father sensed that his son wasn't really going to do anything drastic the next day. He decided that whatever suggestions and advice he was saving for his son became unnecessary. The boy played football with Joe the next day, appropriately handling Joe's shortcomings without being bothered by them.

During the conversation it would have been tempting for the father to advise his son never to hate others or to command him to never again say that he'd kill someone, or to instruct him on ways of handling the situation. However, in this case because of the specific people involved, it "fit" to listen and let the feelings come out so they could subside rather than escalate.

46

Exercise #5

Imagine you are the parent of the child, mentioned in the beginning of this chapter, whose dog was just hit by a car. You have decided to use ARE Listening in responding to your child. Write the phrase or sentence you would communicate under each of the child's statements. (For any statement you cannot determine a feeling response, write a paraphrasing tape recorder response or "um-hmmm.")

"Spot can't die—he can't—he can't!!"

"I don't know what I'd do without him."

"God wouldn't take him away from me—it wouldn't be right."

"Poor Spot, poor Spot."

"He's never been hurt before. He's in such pain."

"I hope he isn't hurting too much."

"He is such a good dog. I love him, I love him."

(crying) "What if he dies? What'll I do?"

"I can't imagine being without him . . . I'll be so lonely."

(screaming) "It's my fault, it's my fault! If I would have just kept him closer to me when we crossed the highway."

"I blew it. I hate myself!"

"Poor Spot, What can I do?"

There are no correct or incorrect responses; however, it is helpful to get feedback on how others respond with ARE Listening. Here are the responses I made to the above exercise:

C: "Spot can't die—he can't, he can't!!"

P: "You are afraid Spot is going to die."

C: "I don't know what I'd do without him."

P: "You would be very lonely without Spot."

C: "God wouldn't take him away from me—it wouldn't be right."

P: "It would seem unfair to you."

C: "Poor Spot, poor Spot."

P: "You feel very sorry for him."

C: "He's never been hurt before. He's in such pain."

P: "You're worried about how much he might be hurting."

C: "I hope he isn't hurting too much."

P: "You care very much about how he is feeling."

C: "He's such a good dog. I love him, I love him."

P: "You love Spot."

C: (crying) "What if he dies? What'll I do?"

P: "You would miss him very much."

C: "I can't imagine being without him . . . I'll be so lonely."

P: "It would be so lonely to be without Spot."

C: (screaming) "It's my fault, it's my fault. If I would have just kept him closer to me when we crossed the highway."

P: "You're upset with yourself for not being more careful."

C: "I blew it. I hate myself!"

P: "You are very angry with yourself."

C: "Poor Spot. Poor Spot. What can I do?"

P: "You want to comfort Spot, but you feel helpless."

In this kind of a situation feelings do not dissipate easily or rapidly. If Spot does not survive, the child may be upset for quite some time to come. ARE Listening cannot remove this life reality, but it can provide support and understanding while leaving the door open for communicating the long lasting pain to someone who cares.

Sometimes it is difficult to think of words that match feelings. Frequently using the terms "angry" or "mad" can begin to seem redundant and may not fit what the individual is trying to express. Below are some of the words that describe unhappy feelings:

grumpy, infuriated, furious, indignant, aghast, afraid, fearful, terrified, scared, gloomy, depressed, frustrated, discouraged, lonely, isolated, concerned, embarrassed, down, depressed sad, cut-off, strung out, disintegrated.

Exercise #6

List below any additional words which describe unhappy feelings that exist in your home or classroom. Ask a child for some suggestions, and you may be amazed at how tuned in children are to feelings. Return to this exercise this week, when you or others you are tuned in to experience feelings that could be added to this list.

There are times when you might also choose to ARE Listen to positive feelings. This could help avoid the liabilities of having intensive and caring reserved only for problem situations. A person likes to share his joys and wonderments with another human being. Communication of cherishing or valuing, increased self-understanding, and positive relationship are but a few of the benefits of ARE Listening to positive feelings. Some words that describe positive feelings are:

happy, glad, excited, elated, love, joy, warmth, wonder, thrilled, proud, accomplished, relieved, high, relaxed, mellow, peaceful, together.

Exercise #7

List below other words you and/or a child can think of (return to this exercise several times this week).

Exercise #8

As in Exercise #3, ask a partner to talk with you about a pet peeve or something that really concerns him or her. If it is difficult to think of something, just talk about a specific child who is having a problem or talk about one's reactions to this book. Your role is to refrain from asking questions and giving advice, instead listen with engrossment and without judgment. Reflect back to your partner with feelings you hear. When you can't hear feelings, respond by saying "um-hmmm" or by paraphrasing.

At the end of the five minutes, ask your partner what it felt like to be listened to in this manner. Discuss with your partner some of the feelings and difficulties you had trying to implement this method of listening. To experience the other end of this communication, ask your partner now to reverse roles with you and try going through the same example used above or an alternate example.

Nurturing Options for Concernable Behavior:

Advising—Instructing—Preventing—Listening

1. Advising or instructing are viable options but often can be more effective after Listening.
2. Preventing can reduce the number of concernable problems.
3. For most concernable problem situations, listening first will help determine if other options are needed—sometimes they are not.
4. ARE Listening—("ARE you Listening?")

   Active (Gordon)   )
   Reflective (Ginott)   ) Listening
   Engrossed and Empathic)

ARE Listening requires:

1. time
2. sincerity
3. caring
4. non-judgment
5. communicating empathy

It's four main elements are:

1. empathic body language
2. um-hmm
3. paraphrasing content
4. reflecting feelings
   a. determine the feeling
   b. find the words to communicate it

ARE Listening, like any other relationship option, has its advantages and disadvantages. Through the exercises in this chapter, you may have developed opinions about ARE Listening and whether or not it is a viable option. List below the advantages that occur to you concerning ARE Listening:

What are the disadvantages of ARE Listening? List below the ones that occur to you:

These answers fit for me:

Advantages:

Gives me something to say in a difficult situation.

Intensifies positive relationships.

Helps relieve feelings.

Provides an emotional mirror.

Increases self-understanding.

Increases independence and maturity.

Sets the stage for problem solving (if a persisting problem is solvable and needs to be solved).

Disadvantages:

Sometimes feels a little awkward.

It doesn't come naturally.

It sometimes seems unfinished.

It is too time consuming to be used much in casual relationships.

It can be overdone—especially when used in situations that would be better handled by another option.

> Example: Child: "Where is the bathroom?"
> Adult: "You are concerned about finding the bathroom."
> Child: "Never mind, I don't need it anymore. But where can I find a mop?"

One of the greatest disadvantages of ARE Listening is that it sometimes seems unfinished. Part of living life without intense anxiety is attempting to accept the lack of closure some elements in life have. Life's problems are not always immediately resolvable. There are also times when the adult could solve a problem for a child but chooses not to, because the child might benefit from finding his or her own solution.

Additionally, there are times when an adult might choose to help a child reach solutions through a process known as "ARE Listening Problem Solving." The main elements in ARE Listening Problem Solving are:

1. ARE Listen to the problem

2. ask the individual for solutions (add your own solutions if needed)

3. decide on a solution

4. implement the solution (with your help if wanted)

Here is an example of a parent utilizing ARE Listening Problem Solving with his son:

S: "Dad, will you go out and beat up Keith?" (Both boys are seven-year-old friends.)

D: "You are really mad at Keith."

S: "I hate him. He's telling everybody that I stole Kathy's ball and put my name on it. They keep calling me names like 'Sticky Stealer.' It's a crummy neighborhood."

D: "The teasing hurts."

S: "It was Keith who told me to put my name on the ball and he says he didn't."

D: "It seems unfair to you."

S: "It is unfair and you should go beat him up."

D: "You want me to take care of it for you but you know I won't. How can the problem be solved?"

S: "You could go tell his mother."

D: "Do you have any other ideas for solving the problem?"

S: "You could talk to Keith."

D: "I could help you and Keith talk together about the problem."

S: (hesitantly) "Okay."

The father had each boy state his view of the problem, requiring each to repeat what he had heard the other say. He asked each to tell the other what he wanted him to do so the problem would stop. Keith said he would stop teasing if the ball were given back to Kathy. It was done and the boys played happily together the rest of the day. Just before they went out to play, the father communicated a few brief words of "advice" about letting friends influence inappropriate behavior and withholding others' property.

ARE Listening and ARE Listening Problem Solving are fairly easy concepts to understand but take a considerable length of time, practice, and experience to become natural extensions of one's relationships with others. The quickest way to become discouraged is to expect oneself to become competent in too short a time. To avoid this, consider the following exercise:

Exercise #9

With a partner role play an ARE Listening problem-solving situation you think you might eventually try with a specific problem a child is having. After the problem is resolved in the role playing situation, switch roles. After each of you have had a turn, the adult and the child discuss how it felt to experience this process in each role.

Exercise #10

1. Take a few days at home or in your classroom to observe the feelings that are being expressed. Think about the words you would use to reflect the feelings. On each day that they occur, list below the feelings and the words you thought of using to reflect them.

2. After you have done the above, select the one family member or class member that you think would be the easiest to ARE Listen to. ARE Listen to some of this individual's moderate concernable problems—save the more intensive concernable problems until you feel fairly comfortable in using this option. If at first it seems quite awkward to ARE Listen, let the individual you have selected know that you are practicing a new skill and would appreciate his or her tolerance and cooperation. List below a few quotes of the ARE Listening responses you tried.

3. After you have done the second step for a few days to a week, begin ARE Listening to the moderate concernable problems of several family members or class members. List below a few quotes of your efforts.

4. When the third step becomes comfortable, begin ARE Listening to some of the intensive concernable problems. List some quotes below.

5. Save ARE Listening Problem Solving until you experience some of the exercises in the next chapter.

Effective Options for Tolerable Behavior

Jack and Zack, seven-year-old twins, are constantly running through the living room. Betty, a 13-year-old, leaves the bathroom in a mess. Bob, a nine-year-old, can't seem to get himself dressed in time for school. Beth and Bill, eight and eleven-year-old siblings, continually argue. Jeff, an 18-year-old who spends most of his time working on his car, leaves grease smudges everywhere he goes in the house.

Tolerable behavior is that which the adult feels needs to change but can be endured for the moment. Whether a behavior is tolerable or intolerable is dependent on the level of tolerability of the adult and the circumstances in which the behavior occurs (as discussed in Chapters 3 and 4).

Which of the above behaviors would you describe as tolerable, if they occurred within your home with only immediate family members present? Are there any you would describe as intolerable?

Exercise #1

What action would you take in response to each of the behaviors listed in paragraph 1? Return to this exercise after finishing this chapter to see if your reactions would still be the same (Column 3).

Behavior	What I Would Do	Write "same" or list what you would do differently (save this column for the for the end of chapter)
Jack and Zack running through the living room.		
Betty leaving the bathroom in a mess		
Bob not getting dressed in time.		
Jeff leaving grease smudges throughout the house		

While there are no right or wrong answers to Exercise #1, a nurturing adult might often desire to expand the level of tolerability so that the more "autocratic" options can be reserved, mostly, for the intolerable behaviors. When not overused, selected attention (Enforcer) and/or just telling a child what to do and what not to do (Commander) can be quick and effective ways to respond to tolerable behavior. However, if overused, these options can lose their effectiveness and place a strain on the adult/child relationships. They also could tend to remove the opportunity for the child to grow in his or her self-responsibility.

Therefore, it is important to be sensitive to the effectiveness of, and the level of comfort you have, in the implementation of adult centered options you use for tolerable behavior. If you determine an adult centered option is becoming ineffective because of overuse or uncomfortable feelings or vibrations between you and a child, you may want to consider some of the more child centered options.

The "child-centered" options for tolerable behavior that could be effective and nurturing in most situations are: Preventer, Relinquisher, Confronter and Negotiator. The Preventer option would apply to tolerable behavior in the same way as discussed in the chapter on intolerable behavior. The Relinquisher option would occasionally apply to those behaviors that are a "stage" the child is going through and the adult can live with until the child grows out of it. The Confronter and Negotiator options will be discussed in detail following the next exercise.

For those tolerable behaviors when the Preventer or Relinquisher options are not appropriate, the adult might experience the next sequence of options, stopping at any step that seems the most nurturing to the specific situation:

1. Commander—Telling the child to stop doing something or to start doing something. If this is ineffective, try #2.

2. Enforcer—Using selective attention. If this is ineffective, try #3.

3. Confronter—Confronting the child with your feelings about the behavior. If this is ineffective, try #4.

4. Negotiator—Mutual problem solving the situation.

Exercise #2

This exercise is an expansion of a part of Exercises #3 and #4 in the third chapter. You may want to refer to those exercises under the tolerable category for a starter.

In column 1, list all the tolerable behaviors you can think of that occur in your home or in your classroom.

In column 2, list the name of the option you most frequently use for that behavior.

In column 3, put the word "same" if you think you are using the most nurturing option for the behavior. If you think a different option would be more nurturing, list its name.

List of Tolerable Behaviors	Options I Most Frequently Use for Each Behavior	The Most Nurturing Option for the Behavior

For the options you changed in column 3, ask yourself which changes would be presently possible for you to make and which would be presently very difficult.

Confronting as an Option for Tolerable Behavior

The term confrontation as used in this chapter will refer to confronting the child with the feelings an adult has about a behavior. Confrontation is ARE Listening in reverse. Instead of commanding the child to do something, the confronter gets in touch with the feeling evoked by the behavior and, without adding judgment, communicates the feeling to the child.

Confrontation will be referred to as ARE Sending (as in, "Are you clearly sending your feelings?"). The keys to ARE Sending are: owning the feeling, describing the feeling, and describing the action or behavior that evoked the feeling without labeling the child's character or personality. (If a child is labeled often enough he or she will begin to live up to the label.)

When a child behaves in a way that is not totally acceptable to an adult, the type and intensity of feeling the adult experiences is affected by his or her personality, background, and perceptions. Keeping this in mind may help the emphasis of ARE Sending to be on helping the child to respect and make room for the feelings of the adult. The nurturer tries to communicate to the child: (1) this is a feeling that comes from me, (2) when this behavior occurs, (3) the feeling is connected with the behavior and not with your personality.

The outline below might tie these concepts together for you:

ARE Sending ("Are you clearly sending your feelings?").

Keys to ARE Sending:

1. Owning the feeling.
2. Stating the feeling.
3. Describing the action or behavior without labeling the child.

The adult tries to communicate:

1. This is a feeling that comes from me—
2. when this behavior occurs.
3. The feeling is connected with the behavior and not with your personality.

Following are some examples of ARE Sending messages that might have been used for the behaviors described in the first paragraph of this chapter. The feeling selected for each example is one among many possibilities.

Jack and Zack are constantly running in the living room:

The Feeling Owned by the Adult	*The Behavior*
Worried that something may break.	Running.

ARE Sending Message
"I'm worried that this running will cause something to get broken."

Betty, a 13-year-old, leaves the bathroom in a mess:

The Feeling Owned by the Adult	*The Behavior*
Embarrassment (when others visit and see the mess).	Leaving a mess.

ARE Sending Message
"I get embarrassed when others see the mess the bathroom is left in."

Beth and Bill, 8 and 11-year-old siblings, continually argue:

The Feeling Owned by the Adult	*The Behavior*
Fear (that they will wind up hating each other).	Continual arguing

ARE Sending Message
"When this arguing goes on continually, I fear that you'll forget that you love each other."

Jeff, an 18-year-old who spends most of his free time working on his car, leaves grease smudges everywhere he goes in the house:

The Feeling Owned by the Adult	*The Behavior*
Irritation (at the deterioration of the house and furniture).	Smudging.

ARE Sending Message
"When I see the walls and furniture smudged with grease, it really irritates me." or "I really get irritated when I see another grease smudge on the wall or on the furniture."

The above examples could vary considerably, depending on the feelings of the adult. However, their general structure would remain the same, i.e., the sentence would usually start with "I" or "when" and include the adult's feeling and the behavior that evoked it without labeling the child.

The child might not clearly understand the feeling the adult is experiencing unless it is stated with the same degree of emotion as is felt. If the feeling is intense and the adult states it calmly and softly, the impact of the statement may be ineffective. Children are not hurt by adults raising their voices and stating feelings with realistic emphasis. In fact, they are often relieved to understand definite feelings connected with behavior, rather than wondering about some lingering, unverbalized, uncomfortable vibrations between adult and child.

However, the adult could overshoot in this area, if he or she unloaded a lot of emotions that are not directly connected with what the child has done. If you have had a bad day at work or with your spouse, etc. and haven't been able to get those feelings out, there is the danger of unjustly dumping the whole load of emotions on the one person you have an opportunity to confront. If this happens, it is often helpful to take the first calm moment following an outburst to explain to the child why you overreacted.

The main purposes of ARE Sending are:

1. to allow the child to accept realistic responsibility for behavior
2. to develop consideration for the feelings of others.

Other purposes include:

1. providing a mature model for the child in expressing feelings
2. clearing the air so that child understands more clearly how the adult feels
3. relieving the immediate feelings of the adult so that they do not build up and cause an "explosion" of feeling that is too much for the child to handle
4. clarifying that the feelings are connected to behavior instead of personality
5. setting the stage for mutual problem solving

Getting in touch with one's own feelings is the most difficult, and yet the most important, part of ARE Sending. Before doing the exercise on the following page, you may want to review some of the words used to describe feelings in the preceding chapter.

58

Exercise #3

Using the list of tolerable behaviors in Exercise #2, complete the following:

Write the feeling owned by you.	List the behavior.	Write an ARE Sending message.

Through ARE Sending some tolerable behaviors will decrease enough so that they are no longer a problem. For those that continue to be a problem, the "Negotiator" option may become a viable way to reach a solution.

The Negotiator uses mutual problem-solving to find solutions to problems. Mutual problem solving has seven steps.

The Seven "A's" of Mutual Problem Solving
1. ARE Send
2. ARE Listen
3. Adjust
4. Ask for solutions
5. Add solutions
6. Agree
7. Act

For more information on ARE Sending, refer to Ginott,[1] *Between Parent and Child,* pgs. 50-52, *Between Parent and Teenager,* pgs. 91-110 and Gordon,[2] *Parent Effectiveness Training,* pgs. 194-264.

Here is an example of utilizing these steps to resolve a problem. The adults (in this case, both parents) were concerned with their eight-and-a-half-year-old son getting to bed on time and getting to sleep early enough so he wouldn't be tired and irritable most of his waking hours. (A = parent responses and C = child's responses.)

ARE Send

In this step, the concerned party communicates his or her perception of the problem and the feelings evoked by the problem.

> A: "I am concerned about a problem that has to be solved. But I want to find a solution that both you and I can live with. I am worried about how long it takes you to get to bed and get to sleep at night. We have a hard time getting you up in the morning and we get irritated when you are grumpy most of the day because of being tired. How do you feel about the problem?"

ARE Listen

In this step the adult(s) ARE Listen to the feelings of the child (no matter how far out his feelings may seem). The only exception to this is if the child wanders from the subject at hand. When this happens, the adult brings the child back to the problem being discussed.

> C: "I just can't get to sleep when I go to bed at 8:00. I just lie there and toss and turn."
>
> A: "It's really hard for you to get to sleep."
>
> C: "Yeah. I keep thinking about all the things that happened in school and the things that are going to happen the next day."
>
> A: "Thinking about school kind of winds you up and makes it hard to relax and sleep."
>
> C: It doesn't seem like there has been enough time for the other things I'd like to do by the time I finish with school and homework."
>
> A: "You would like to have more time for other things."
>
> C: "Yeah. I hardly ever get a chance to see my favorite TV programs. Most of them are after 8:00. Besides most of my friends get to see them. I'm the only one on the street my age that goes to bed so early."
>
> A: "It doesn't seem fair to you."
>
> C: "It isn't fair! And, besides, I never get to sleep before 9:30 anyway."
>
> A: "It upsets you that you don't get to stay up and it doesn't seem to make sense because you can't get to sleep anyway."
>
> C: "Yeah."
>
> A: "Are there any other feelings you have about this that you haven't said yet?"
>
> C: "My bedtime is too close to Bill's (his younger brother). He's always

bugging me! I'm two-and-a-half years older than him and get to stay up only a half-hour later than him. I should have a chance to see some of my programs without him.''

A: "Bill irritates you and you'd like to have some more time to yourself."

C: "Yeah."

Adjust

In this step, the adult restates the problem with any modifications or adjustments necessitated by new perceptions related to what the child has said. This is also the time the adult sends any new feelings that have developed during the discussion. Misperceptions might also be clarified at this time, if things were said by the adult or child that appear to be inaccurate.

A: "It sounds like the bedtime problem is connected with a lack of time to unwind and being able to do something without Bill. We would feel irresponsible if we let you do things just because you have friends who do them. But we do want to find a solution that fits your needs and our needs."

Ask for Solutions

In this step, the adult asks the child for ideas for solutions without initially placing any judgment on the solutions. If more than one child is participating, the children are told not to criticize any solutions suggested by any of the participants during this step. This is particularly important for the child who may be a little timid about making suggestions.

A: "What ideas do you have for a solution to this problem?"

C: "That I not have any bedtime and just go to bed when I'm tired."

A: "That's one idea, do you have any other solutions?"

C: "That I have a 9:30 bedtime, except when something special is happening—then I would stay up a little later."

A: "Umhmm, any other ideas?"

C: "No."

Add Solutions

In this step, the adult adds any solutions he or she has thought of. At this point, the solutions offered are still not to be judged or compared.

A: "Another solution would be for you to get completely ready for bed (snacks, pajamas, etc.) before 9:00 and then go to bed at 9:00."

Agree

In this step, all solutions are compared and evaluated on a basis of what everybody involved could live with. If no solution is acceptable, a time is set for another problem solving session the next day or so for the purpose of "brainstorming" some more solutions. In mutual problem-solving the door is always open for further negotiation, if the problem is not solved or does not stay solved.

A: "Do you see any of the solutions we've discussed as ones that you can't live with?"

C: "I could live with any of them. I like the 9:00 o'clock one the least, but it would be a lot better than what I have now."

A: "Knowing what time you have to get up to go to school and the amount of sleep you usually need, I couldn't live with a 9:30 bedtime until some time in the future when your body doesn't need as much rest. If you went to bed when you felt tired I would worry that there would be plenty of times when you wouldn't be in touch with how tired you were, because you were into something you were really enjoying. If you were really able to go directly to bed at 9:00 and get to sleep more quickly than you do now, I would be very happy with the arrangement. I could live with the 9:00 o'clock solution. Can you make a commitment to really try to make it work?"

C: "Yes, I'll make sure that I'm ready exactly at 9:00 excepting on special nights that I have permission to stay up later."

Act

In this step, the arrangements for implementing the solution are decided (when, where, who, how, etc.).

A: "Let's try the solution for two weeks and then talk about whether it's working."

C: "Okay."

A: "In order to be in bed at 9:00, you should start getting your pajamas on by 8:30 and do all your last snacking and going to the bathroom between 8:30 and 9:00 (perhaps during the 8:45 TV commercial). I'll come into your room at 9:00 to say prayers with you and tuck you in. Is there anything you would like me to do to help us live up to our new solution?"

C: "Would you remind me at 8:45 that the time is getting close?"

A: "I would rather you would be able to do that part on your own but if you think it will help, I'll remind you when it looks like you've lost track of time."

C: "Okay."

In this case, the solution was found to be effective at the end of the two-week trial period.* It continued to be a good solution to all concerned for about two years. The total time taken to solve the problem was about fifteen minutes.

The time needed for mutual problem solving would vary considerably, depending on the nature of the problem and the people involved. Some mutual problem sessions have to be extended into several meetings, sometimes

---

*For another example of a parent and child mutual problem solving, see Gordon,[2] pgs. 209-212. It is a beautiful tape script of a five-year-old girl and her mother resolving a problem.

covering a span of a few days or weeks. Occasionally a problem may not be solvable, but the mutual problem-solving process may still help relieve feelings and leave the hope for finding a solution sometime in the future. Generally, the initial time needed for the Negotiator option is longer than with the more autocratic options but usually, in the long run, the total time and adult energy needed is less because the adult power isn't continually needed to control the behavior.

Adult power is used sparingly in the Negotiator option. It is saved basically for maintaining the structure of the mutual problem solving sessions (sometimes through enforcing or commanding), and occasionally enforcing the implementation of a solution (if all parties agree that a nurturing consequence is needed, it is often the adult that enforces the agreed upon consequence).

Exercise #4

With a partner, discuss a tolerable problem a specific child has that you think would continue in spite of consistent ARE Sending. Tell your partner how you think the child feels about the problem and how he or she might react to a mutual problem-solving session.

Role-play the seven steps of the mutual problem-solving process with your partner. Your partner should react the way the child might react, while you react the way you think you would in the actual situation.

When you have completed the mutual problem solving exercise with your partner, ask him or her how it felt to be the child in this process. Ask yourself how it felt to be the adult. Discuss what things were helpful and what either of you could have done to improve the process. Repeat the exercise, reversing roles.

If more practice is needed before actually doing this with a child or with a group, try Exercise #3 again with some other tolerable behaviors.

Mutual problem solving can be utilized with individuals, small groups (several family members or a group within the classroom), larger groups (the whole family or classroom), or very large groups (all the children in the neighborhood, all the children who ride bikes to school). However, it is advisable when first trying mutual problem solving to start with just one person and a fairly easy problem, saving the more difficult situations for a later time when you feel more familiar and comfortable with this process.

The emphasis of mutual problem solving is neither adult centered nor child centered, it is relationship centered; based on developing mutual respect for each unique human being in the relationship. Lines of rights or power are not drawn. The real power lies in the provision that solution is accepted only if it can be "lived with" by all concerned. Through this, children can become considerate of the tolerabilities of adults and an adult can become sensitive to the degree of independence for which a child is ready.

In many situations, child-centered options can be used in place of, or in combination with, adult-centered options for the purposes of long-term effectiveness and relationship building. The child-centered options do not always have as immediate an effect as the adult-centered options. Because tolerable behavior does not need to change immediately, patience in combination with consistent use of these options is usually growth producing for the child, the adult, and their relationship. Occasionally, there may be a tolerable behavior that does not change through the extended use of child centered options. When this happens, the behavior usually becomes intolerable, which opens up the possibility of moving towards the left on the Range of Nurturing Options on page 15.

The Forces Within Us and Around Us

Six-year-old Bob Jones has spilled milk all over the breakfast table for the fifth time this week. Mr. Jones turns to Mrs. Jones and says, "When are you going to teach your son some table manners?" Mrs. Jones is very proud of the fact that she keeps the house impeccably clean. She looks at the milk dripping on the floor that she had scrubbed again last night. Her feelings of frustration and infuriation well up inside her as she screams at her son, "You are the clumsiest kid I've ever seen. Since you can't be considerate of the rest of us, you'll eat all your meals in the back yard for one month!" As Bob leaves the table with his head down, his mother's irritation and anger turn to guilt. She asks herself, "Why can't I react to these situations the way I think I should?"

The Rodriguez family has recently moved from the town they lived in for the past twenty years. Mr. Rodriguez misses his home town and isn't too sure how the new job he has is going to work out. Dora, his 16-year-old daughter, has often come to him to talk about any problems that are concerning her since he usually is a "good listener." With tears in her eyes Dora says to her father, "I really miss my old friends. I'm so lonely out here." Mr. Rodriguez responds by saying, "Why don't you stop feeling sorry for yourself and go out and make some new friends?" Dora runs into her room, slams the door and cries. Mr. Rodriguez wonders why he reacted the way he did.

Mr. Green, a fifth-grade teacher, has a very active and noisy class this year. He has always taken pride in his ability to deal with classroom behavior. With this particular group he has found that if he calmly and patiently takes action without many words, the children respond positively. Today the principal has been in the classroom to observe Mr. Green as part of his annual evaluation. It has been the noisiest, most active day the class has had in a long time. As the principal leaves the room, Mr. Green turns to the class and says, "This is the most unruly, disrespectful class I have ever seen. If you do not sit down and shut up, I'll give you something to really talk about!" The class is now quiet for the moment, but Mr. Green is not happy with himself. He knows several options that would have been better to use in this situation.

In each of these situations described there were forces happening within and/or around the adult that influenced a less than ideal reaction. When one frequently reacts differently to a child than one means to, it is likely that there is something happening within the person or situation that blocks the use of the options preferred by the adult. Knowledge and experience with relationship and discipline options are not always enough. Increasing "self-understanding" and "situational understanding" can be helpful.

The search for self-understanding is complex and unending. Getting in touch with some of the forces within oneself can be an effective step in the direction of matching (or separating, when necessary) our inner feelings from our outer reactions.

There is much that goes on inside of us that is affected by our life experiences, the things we value most, and the things that are important to us. One way to start to get in touch with these forces within us is to ask the following questions:

What do I value most in life?

What is the greatest personal need I have?

How much confidence do I have in others to do the right thing?

How secure do I feel as a parent? How secure do I feel as a person? Where do my feelings of security come from—Self? Others? Both?

How do I usually react to stress or conflict situations with adults? With children? Do I overract? Underreact? Become dominant? Become submissive?

Where have my relationship and discipline choices come from (how my parents related to me? Seeing my friends discipline their children? Other situations?)

Exercise #1

On the chart below, write one or two thoughts for each of the above questions.

FORCES WITHIN ME*

Value

Personal Need

*Thanks to Richard Schmuck[5] as the author's original source for this concept and the concept explored at the end of the chapter.

Security

Confidence in Others

Stress and Conflict Reactions

Origin of Relationship and Discipline Choices

Understanding the situations in which we find ourselves is also a complex and unending task. As with self-understanding, situational understanding can be enhanced by taking a look at the forces within the situation.

The forces within a situation can often influence both your inner feelings and outer reactions. Your family or school situtation, the number of responsibilities you have, the time you have to fulfill them, the response others give to your decisions, what others expect of you, and the vibrations (feeling tone, mutual respect, etc.) within your family or school can strongly affect the relationship and discipline options you use. The more clearly one is in touch with these forces, the more effective one can be in shaping them to become conducive to positive relationship. To begin to become more closely in touch with these forces, ask yourself the following questions:

What have been the main options used for influencing one another within my family or school?

What expectations do my family members or school staff have of me? Do they match my self-expectations?

How many roles and responsibilities am I attempting to fulfill?

Is time a problem?

What influence do my decisions and reactions have?

What is the general feeling tone and level of respect that exists between family or staff members?

Exercise #2

On the chart beginning on the next page, write one or two thoughts for each of the above questions.

FORCES WITHIN THE SITUATION

Family or school staff options of influence:

_____

Expectations others have of me:

_____

Roles and responsibilities:

_____

Time:

_____

Influence of my decisions and reactions:

_____

Family or staff feeling tone and mutual respect:

_____

There is one specific element in the situation in which we find ourselves that merits a closer look—the significant others in one's family or school. The values, needs, and assumed roles the other adults in the situation can have a strong effect on one's own reactions. It may be helpful to ask the significant others in the situation to do the previous two exercises and discuss the similarities and differences.

Among the significant others in one's family or school, children are of particular importance. Each child has his or her individual way of reacting to the relationship and discipline of the adult. The adult's reactions, patience, and level of tolerance can be strongly influenced by this. It may be helpful to take a close look at a specific child to consider the degree of influence his or her reactions have on the forces within self and the situation. Ask yourself the following questions about a specific child:

What expectations (roles, reactions, etc.) does the child have of me?

To which relationship and discipline options does the child most readily respond?

What options does the child use in his or her relationships with others?

Are the options the child receives or uses the best ones for the situation and people involved?

What needs does the child have of me, others, and self?

How does the child handle responsibility?

How secure is the child in situations of stress, conflict, or ambiguity?

What does the child value most in life at this time?

How is the child's self-esteem (positive, low, inbetween)?

Exercise #3

On the chart beginning on the next page, list a couple of thoughts for each of the above questions. (You may want to talk with the child about this exercise.)

FORCES WITHIN THE CHILD

Child's expectations of the adult:

Child's responsiveness to relationship and discipline options:

Options the child uses with others:

Quality of the options that work with the child:

Quality of the options the child uses with others:

Child's needs of self, others, and the adult:

Child's responsibility tolerance:

Child's security:

Child's values:

Child's self-esteem:

In taking a look at the fields of force within our lives, we become aware that the forces within us, within our situation, and within significant others are not always in harmony with one another. Within the nurturer's life span there can be a field of forces that are often in conflict. The struggle between the forces within our lives can produce many dilemmas, a few of which are listed below:

Dilemmas We Face

Positive Force		Distracting Force
We value people	and yet	we spend much of our time with things.
We want love, acceptance, and feelings of accomplishment	and yet	we habitually give more attention to aversive attributes than to positive ones.
We realize freedom is usually non-existent without responsibility, commitment, and sacrifice	and yet	we are tempted to make freedom a gift to children.
The child's readiness for responsibility develops over the years	and yet	we want the child to behave and respond responsibly now.
We usually are aware of the options that are best for our situation	and yet	when we are rushed, tired, or under stress our immediate reactions often leave us feeling guilty.
We strive to increase our level of tolerance	and yet	we find old feelings and reactions quietly sift back into our present behavior.
We are able to use the options we feel are appropriate	and yet	we sometimes find them to be in conflict with the options used by the significant others in the child's environment.
We find it possible to be consistent with our options when the conflicts or problems are not too far out	and yet	when we need rational consistency the most, we have it the least.
We need to be nurturing of ourselves in order to have the strength and energy to nurture others	and yet	what we and others expect of us seldom leaves any time for self.
We become somewhat consistent in our options with one child	and yet	find the same options may not be the best for another child.

We want children to be cooperative	and yet	we have a cultural tradition of competition and aggressiveness.
We strive for perfection in our relationships with others	and yet	imperfection is a part of humanness.
We want to solve all of life's problems	and yet	not all problems are resolvable.
We want our closest relationships to be filled with happiness and contentment	and yet	Intimacy includes both the joys and disappointments of relationship.

Exercise #4

Keeping in mind your responses to Exercises #1-#3, add a few dilemmas that you face:

Positive Force	and yet	Distracting Force

Resolving the Dilemmas We Face

The dilemmas we face are not always irresolvable. Being in touch with the forces in our lives enhances the possibility of redirecting some of those forces for positive change. One method to redirect forces is to take a look at the "force field." This particular method is based on Kurt Lewin's, "Force Field Analysis," and is adapted from the NTL Institue of Washington, D.C.

The force field is all the forces that maximize and minimize the possibilities of solving a problem or conflict. A force field could be illustrated as follows:

FORCE FIELD

Forces----	C	----Forces
	H	
for ----	A	----against
	N	
Change --	G	----Change
	E	

When your force field is interfering with the utilization of the relationship and discipline options you prefer, the following approach may be helpful:

1. List the problem.
2. List the changes you would like to make.
3. List the forces for change.
4. List the forces against change.
5. Underline the forces for change that are the most important and possible for you to increase.
6. Underline the forces against change that are the most important and possible for you to decrease.
7. Brainstorm (list spontaenously without judging) the actions you will take to reduce the forces against change and increase the forces for change.

73

8. Underline the actions you feel are the most effective and practical to start with.
9. List the underlined actions into a plan with specific time commitments for starting each action.

Below is an example of a force field analysis:

Problem

When I'm irritable and upset, I "blast off" in a way that seems threatening to others in my family.

Change Desired

To use ARE Sending in these situations.

Forces for Change	Forces Against Change
I know how to ARE Send.	I have a natural tendency to "blast off."
I feel better when I use it.	My feelings tend to build up and then uncontrollably come out all at once.
I value honest confrontation.	
My family responds much better to ARE Sending than to just plain grouchiness.	I am often tired during the hours that I am home.
	I have a lot of things to do and very little time to do them.
	I often "blast off" when listening to others would be more effective.

Example of brainstorming actions for reducing or increasing forces.

Increasing forces for change:

Practice ARE Sending by using it in less tense situations.

Keep a count of the number of times a week I ARE Send (and/or ARE Listen if the other person is experiencing intense feelings) instead of uncontrollably "blasting off."

Reread books that discuss ARE Sending.

Attend a class or group that is emphasizing ARE Sending.

Let my family members know that I'm trying to improve in this area and that I would like them to help me keep track of when I am ARE Sending and when I am just "blasting off."

Decreasing forces against change:

Keep in touch with the minor negative feelings I have each day and find a way to to get them out immediately so they won't build up.

Change my priorities at work and at home so that I have time for myself and family.

Arrange to have very little to do between dinner and the children's bedtime so I can relax and be available to them.

Find a way to "talk out" any daily accumulation of aversive feelings.

Plan of Action	When
I will practice ARE Sending mentally by thinking of the words I should have used in place of a "blast off."	Starting tomorrow during the time that I calm down after each "blast off."
I will carry a 3x5 card in my pocket and put a checkmark in one column for each time I ARE Send and put a checkmark in a second column for each time I "blast off."	I'll purchase a packet of cards during my lunch hour tomorrow and begin counting tomorrow evening.
I'll hold a family meeting during dinner-time, asking for their suggestions and support.	One week from tomorrow.
Have a special conversation time with my wife before dinner so I can talk out any of the aversive feelings that remain from the day's experiences.	Starting tomorrow.
Do all reading, writing, and leftover work either before dinner or after the children go to bed so I can relax and enjoy them.	Starting tomorrow evening.

One problem that is common to many adults is the time needed versus the time available for nurturing. Conflicting demands on our time is often a constant reality in our present society, yet one of the most important ingredients in nurturing is time. The excerpt on the following page, from an anonymous source, illustrates this meaningfully.

Mystery of Time

TIME.

It hangs heavy for the bored, eludes the busy, flies by for the young and runs out for the aged.

TIME.

We talk about it like it's a manufactured commodity that some can afford, others can't; some can reproduce, others waste.

We crave it. We curse it. We kill it. We abuse it. Is it a friend? Or an enemy? I suspect we know very little about it. To know it at all, and its potential, perhaps we should view it through a child's eyes.

"When I was young, Daddy was going to throw me up in the air and catch me and I would giggle until I couldn't giggle anymore, but he had to change the furnace filter, and there wasn't time."

76

"When I was young, Mama was going to read me a story and I was going to turn the pages and pretend I could read, but she had to wax the bathroom floor and there wasn't time."

"When I was young, Daddy was going to come to school and watch me in a play. I was the fourth Wise Man (in case one of the three got sick), but he had an appointment to have his car tuned up and it took longer than he thought and there was no time."

"When I was young, Grandma and Granddad were going to come for Christmas to see the expression on my face when I got my first bike, but Grandma didn't know who she could get to feed the dogs and Granddad didn't like the cold weather and besides, they didn't have the time."

"When I was young, Mama was going to listen to me read my essay on 'What I Want to Be When I Grow Up,' but she was in the middle of the Monday Night Movie and Gregory Peck was always one of her favorites and there wasn't time."

"When I was older, Dad and I were going fishing one weekend, just the two of us, and we were going to pitch a tent and fry fish with the heads on them like they do in the flashlight ads, but at the last minute he had to fertilize the grass and there wasn't time."

"When I was older, the whole family was always going to pose together for our Christmas card, but my brother had ball practice, my sister had her hair up, Dad was watching the Colts and Mom had to wax the bathroom floor. There wasn't time."

"When I grew up and left home to be married, I was going to sit down with Mom and Dad and tell them I loved them and I would miss them. But Hank—he's my best man and a real clown—was honking the horn in front of the house, so there wasn't time."

Exercise #1

If time is a problem for you, see if completing the following Force Field analysis is helpful. (Change the statement of the problem and the change wanted, if it doesn't fit you.)

Problem

I have difficulty implementing my best relationship and discipline options because it's hard to take the time away from other activities.

Change Desired

To increase the amount and/or quality of time I have for relationship and nurturing discipline with my children or classroom.

Forces Against Change	Forces for Change

Underline the forces for change that are the most important and possible for you to increase.

Underline the forces against change that are the most important and possible for you to decrease.

Brainstorm actions to increase the underlined forces for change and decrease the underlined forces against change.

Increasing forces for change:

Decreasing forces against change:

Underline those actions you feel are the most effective and practical to start with.

Using the underlined actions, list a plan of action:

Plan of Action	When

Another problem that is common to many adults is finding that there is a conflict between what one would like to tolerate in children and what one actually does tolerate. It is often difficult to perceive with realistic objectivity child behaviors that worry or concern us. Sometimes it is a matter of one's perspective as the following letter indicates:[2]

College of Fine Arts, Albany, New York

Dear Mother and Dad:

It has been three months since I left for college. I have been remiss in writing and I am very sorry for my thoughtlessness in not having written before. But, before you read this, please sit down, OK?

Well, I am getting along pretty well now. The skull fracture and the concussion I got when I jumped out of the window of my dormitory when it caught on fire shortly after my arrival are pretty well healed now. I only spent two weeks in the hospital and now I can see almost normally and get those sick headaches only once in awhile.

Fortunately, the fire in the dormitory and my jump were witnessed by an attendant at the gas station near the dorm and he was the one who called the fire department and the ambulance. He also visited me at the hospital and since I had nowhere to live because of the burned out dorm, he was kind enough to invite me to share his apartment with him. He is a very fine person and we have fallen deeply in love and are planning to get married. We haven't set the date yet, but it will be before my pregnancy begins to show.

Yes, Mother and Dad, I am pregnant. I know how much you are looking forward to being grandparents and I know you will welcome the baby and give it the same love and devotion and tender care you gave me when I was a child. The reason for the delay in our marriage is that my boyfriend has some minor infection which prevents us from passing our premarital blood tests and I carelessly caught it from him. This will soon clear up with the penicillin injections I am now taking daily.

Now that I have brought you up to date, I want to tell you that there was no dormitory fire, I did not have a concussion or a skull fracture, I was not in the hospital, I am not pregnant, I am not engaged, I do not have syphilis and there is no one in my life. However, I am getting a "D" in History and an "F" in Science, and I wanted you to see these marks in their proper perspective.

Your Loving Daughter,

Exercise #2

If tolerance is a problem for you*, use steps 1-9 on page 73 to complete the following Force Field analysis. (Change the statement of the problem and the change desired, if it doesn't fit you.)

Problem

I find myself overreacting to behaviors that I think I want to be more tolerant of.

Change Desired

To raise my level of tolerance and acceptance.

Forces for Change	Forces Against Change

Underline the forces for change that are the most important and possible for you to increase.

Underline the forces against change that are the most important and possible for you to decrease.

---

*Being in touch with the stages that age groups generally go through during childhood can often be helpful to adult tolerability. See reference 16.

Brainstorm actions to increase the underlined forces for change and decrease the underlined forces against change.

Increasing forces for change:

Decreasing forces against change:

Underline those actions you feel are the most effective and practical to start with.

Using the underlined actions, list a plan of action:

Plan of Action	When

There are many problems that are common to adults who aspire to be nurturing of children. Being inconsistent, focusing on aversive behavior, using non-productive consequences, forgetting to cherish, advising before listening, are but a few.

Exercise #3

Using a problem that exists in your situation or one of the dilemmas mentioned in the previous chapter, complete this Force Field analysis.

Problem

Change Desired

Forces for Change	Forces Against Change

Underline the forces for change that are the most important and possible for you to increase.

Underline the forces against change that are the most important and possible for you to decrease.

82

Brainstorm actions to increase the underlined forces for change and decrease the underlined forces against change.

Increasing forces for change:

Decreasing forces against change:

Underline those actions you feel are the most effective and practical to start with.

Using the underlined actions, list a plan of action:

Plan of Action	When

While Force Field analysis can be very helpful in dealing with some of the dilemmas nurturers face, there are times when implementing a force field plan of action can be very difficult. When there is extreme difficulty it often can be because of one or more of the following three factors:

1. The nurturer has given priority to everything but self.
2. The nurturer has set unrealistic self-expectations.
3. The nurturer needs a deeper understanding of the forces within self.

Including Self in One's List of Priorities

While adults often become parents and/or teachers because they want to share life with children, it is easy to forget that you cannot share unless there is something left in you to share. When we run out of time, energy, peaceful moments, and enjoyment for self, the well from which we draw begins to run dry. Because of this, no matter how many responsibilities we have or how much is expected of us, finding some time for self each day is a necessity. No force field plan of action that totally intrudes on the moments that we have set aside for ourselves can be effective over an extended period of time. If you find that your plans of action often leave no room for your own enjoying life, consider the following as a possible beginning for a Force Field analysis:

Problem

Having so many "shoulds" in life that there is no time to cultivate my own excitements and interests.

Change Desired

To balance each day so that there is room for self as well as others.

Setting Realistic Self-Expectations

As nurturers we seem to understand that change in others is often a gradual, evolving process. We delight in the step-by-step progress (even when it's three steps forward and two steps backward) in children. We are aware that set behavior habits are difficult to change. We give children considerable patience, continuing positive support, and frequent reminders that they are progressing to help reverse behavior problems. But when we decide we want to change our own behaviors or habits, we feel guilty if we do not change immediately. Adults, too, need from themselves and others patience, positive support, and frequent reminders of progress.

A realistic force field plan of action needs expectations to be within the present capability of the adult and a built-in system of reminders (check cards, appreciation from others, etc.) of the gradual approximations of positive change.

Clearer Understanding of the Forces Within Self

Force Field analysis deals mainly with the forces at or near the surface of our functioning. When we continue to have difficulty functioning well in spite of wanting and trying hard to resolve our problems, there may be deeper forces within us which inhibit change.

Getting in touch with, and resolving, the deeper forces within us is a difficult but attainable desire. We have many resources within our environment for increasing deeper self-understanding—two are books on self-understanding and professional counseling.

Professional counseling is a process through which a "normal" person can increase in maturity and self-understanding at a much faster rate than through individual effort. It is not usually necessary to go through years of therapy to accomplish this; ten sessions of counseling often can produce as much growth as several years of "trying and experiencing" on your own. Most communities provide counseling agencies that charge anywhere from nothing to a rate adjusted to fit a family's financial needs; for those who can afford private counselors, the cost for ten sessions is usually less than a TV set.

If you are interested in exploring the possibility of counseling, a list of your area's counseling services can be provided by a school psychologist, your county Health Department, a minister, or your phone book (look under Family Service Association, family counselors, or the county Mental Health Clinic, etc.).

If you do not see counseling as a present alternative, reading a book on self-understanding and discussing your reading experience with a person who cares and is a good listener, might be an approach you want to consider. Books I found helpful in understanding the forces within myself are, *I'm OK, You're OK*,[5] by Tom Harris, *People Making*,[4] by Virginia Satir and *Born to Win*,[18] by Muriel James and Dorothy Jongeward. Books on the subjects of meditation, visualization, fantasy, and dreams have also been very helpful.

The list of good books in this area is endless. Browsing through the psychology section of a library or a book store could expose to you enough self-enhancing books to last a lifetime.

In our modern, pluralistic society where the only thing that is constant is change, the old saying, "The only thing I can be sure about is me and thee . . . and I'm not too sure about thee" takes on a special meaning. Though it is important to be aware of and work on the forces around us, it is the forces within us which ultimately have the most influence.

Parting Thoughts

It is hoped that this book has helped you to determine the nurturing options that best enhance the growth and development of the children in your life, for children are apprentice adults, and will become an extension of the nurturing experiences to which they are exposed.

While children are apprentice adults they are not apprentice human beings. They have been human beings since they first existed. If they can be nurtured with the respect that is the birthright of human beings of all ages, they can achieve one of the major goals of life itself:

To Give and Receive Love

May your life and the lives of those around you be filled with caring, meaningful, real LOVE!

References

1. Ginot, Haim. *Between Parent and Child*. New York: The MacMillan Co., 1965.

_____. *Between Parent and Teenager*. New York: The MacMillan Co., 1969.

2. Gordon, Thomas. *Parent Effectiveness Training*. New York: Peter H. Wyden, Inc., 1970.

3. Patterson, Gerald R. *Families*. Champaign, Ill. Research Press Co., 1971.

_____. *Living with Children*. Champaign, Ill. Research Press Co., 1971.

4. Satir, Virginia. *People Making*. Palo Alto, California: Science and Behavior Books, Inc., 1972.

5, Schmuck, Richard A. and Matthew Miles. *Organizational Development in Schools*. Palo Alto, Ca.: National Press Books, 1971.

6. Briggs, Dorothy Corkville. *Your Child's Self Esteem*. Garden City, N.J.: Doubleday & Company, Inc., 1970.

7. Coopersmith, Stanley. *The Antecedents of Self Esteem*. San Francisco, Ca. W.H. Freeman and Company, 1967.

8. Purkey, William W. *Self Concept and School Achievement*. Englewood Cliffs, N.J.: Prentice-Hall, Inc., 1970.

9. American Greetings Cards.

10. Dreikurs, Rudoph and Pearl Cassel. *Discipline Without Tears*. New York, N.Y.: Hasthorne Books, Inc., 1972.

_____. *A New Approach to Discipline: Logical Consequences*. New York, N.Y.: Hawthorne Books, Inc., 1968.

11. Dodson, Fitzhugh. *How to Parent*. Los Angeles, Ca.: Nash Publishing, 1970.

12. Dobson, James. *Hide and Seek*. Old Tappan, N.J.: Fleming H. Revill Co., 1974.

13. Krumbolt, John D. and Helen B. Krumboltz. *Changing Children's Behavior*. Englewood Cliffs, N.J.: Prentice-Hall, Inc., 1972.

14. Homme, Lloyd. *How to Use Contingency Contracting in the Classroom*. Champaign, Ill.: Research Press Co., 1970.

15. Herbert, Cindy. *I See a Child*. Garden City, N.Y.: Anchor Press/Doubleday & Co., Inc., 1974.

16. Ilg, Frances L. and Louise Bates Ames. *The Gesell Institute's Child Behavior*. New York: Dell Publishing Co., Inc., 1955.

17. Harris, Thomas A. *I'm OK—You're OK*. New York and Evanston: Harper and Row, Publishers, 1967.

18. James, Muriel and Jongeward, Dorothy. *Born to Win*. Menlo Park, Ca.: Addison-Wesley Publishing Company, 1971.